MW00534827

A Beginning Latin
CHRISTIAN READER
De Bonis Cogitationibus

by Rose Williams

Bolchazy-Carducci Publishers, Inc.

Mundelein, Illinois USA

Editor: Donald E. Sprague
Contributing Editor: John C. Traupman
Cover Design & Typography: Adam Phillip Velez

A Beginning Latin Christian Reader
De Bonis Cogitationibus

Rose Williams

© 2010 Bolchazy-Carducci Publishers, Inc.
All rights reserved.

Bolchazy-Carducci Publishers, Inc.
1570 Baskin Road
Mundelein, Illinois 60060
www.bolchazy.com

Printed in the United States of America
2010
by United Graphics

ISBN 978-0-86516-750-6

Library of Congress Cataloging-in-Publication Data

Williams, Rose, 1937-
  A beginning Latin Christian reader : de bonis cogitationibus / by Rose Williams.
    p. cm.
  Includes bibliographical references and index.
  ISBN 978-0-86516-750-6 (pbk. : alk. paper) 1. Latin language--Readers--Christian life.
2. Christian life. 3. Bible--Quotations. I. Title.
  PA2095.W54 2010
  478'.6421--dc22
                                                                    2010021745

TABLE OF CONTENTS

Special Acknowledgement

The author gratefully acknowledges the special assistance and expertise of Dr. John Traupman, who edited the Latinity of the adapted Latin passages.

INTRODUCTION
Dē Bonīs Cōgitātiōnibus

Adapted from Philippians 4:8

Quae sunt vēra, quae sunt pūra, quae sunt iūsta, quae sunt sāncta, quae sunt amābilia, quae sunt fāmae bonae: haec cōgitāte.

Master educator and veteran Latin teacher Rose Williams has authored a beginning Latin Christian reader that will complement any beginning Latin course. She draws thought-provoking readings from the Bible and other Christian sources as well as from some ancient Roman literature. These selections all illuminate the book's central theme, drawn from Philippians 4.8 (see above).

Inspired by Waldo Sweet's innovative reading approach to Latin whose insights Ms. Williams incorporated into her own teaching through the years, she has designed *De Bonis Cogitationibus* to be an ideal complement to *Artes Latinae*. The text, moreover, works well with all introductory Latin texts in addition to those employing the reading method. Each reading is accompanied by an alphabetized vocabulary list. Grammar notes facilitate reading and a set of grammatical appendices provides additional explanations. We recommend that students consult the appendices on an "as needed" basis.

Each section begins with short quotations from the Bible chosen to set the theme of the readings that follow. In the fashion of a graded reader, *De Bonis Cogitationibus* stories are initially short but gradually grow longer and more involved as the student's skills in reading Latin grow. The readings employ classical Latin so that this text will serve as preparation for the beginning Latin student's later transition to more intensive Latin reading.

The readings drawn from the Bible, the Christian fathers, and classical writers will serve as stimuli to discussion as the teacher, parent, homeschooler, and student desire. Ms. Williams has intentionally not provided any commentary or interpretation so that readers can discuss the passages free from an author's bias.

A teacher's guide is available.

For readers desiring a comprehensive review of Latin grammar, Bolchazy-Carducci Publishers recommends Anna Andresian's brilliant *Looking at Latin*, which is available in print or digitally.

DONALD E. SPRAGUE
Editor

SECTION I
Animālia

Adapted from Matthew 7:10

Pater bona dat.
Datne pater vīperam sī fīlius piscem quaerit?

Adapted from Psalm 84:3

Passer domum invenit et hirundō nīdum invenit: sunt altāria tua, Domine Deus.

Adapted from Isaiah 65:25

Agnus et lupus cibum partiunt; leō et taurus herbam partiunt; vīpera pulverem edit. In meō sānctō monte animal nōn occīdit.

Adapted from Numbers 22:21–33

Rēx malus Balaam prophētam vocat. Ad rēgem asina Balaam portat. Asina dēflectit quia angelum in viā videt.

Balaam asinam pūnit. Asina dīcit, "Cūr mē pūnīs?" Balaam dīcit, "Mala es." Asina dīcit, "Nōnne animal tuum sum? Malumne faciō?" "Numquam," Balaam dīcit.

Balaam angelum videt. Angelus dīcit, "Asina mē videt. Asina dēflectit; ergō tū vīvis."

NB: *This story is in the Latin historical present, which means that it can be put in or read as the past tense in English.*

Vocabulary for Introduction and Section I

NB: *In this vocabulary some special helps have been given that will not be found in subsequent vocabularies. In this vocabulary alone the words have been divided into syllables and the stressed syllable for each word has been marked. This will not occur in later vocabularies.*

For a discussion of pronunciation and syllabication, see Appendix I. The English translation for the second form of the noun has been added in this vocabulary to demonstrate that the second form of a noun will always mean "of." Sample sentence: "The eyes of the donkey are bright." For additional explanation of noun endings, see Appendix II.

Also in this vocabulary list, the verb form used in the stories has been given in addition to the traditional dictionary forms. For additional explanation of verb endings, see Appendix II.

ag' nus *m* lamb **ag' nī** of the lamb

al tā' ri a *n pl* altar **al tā' ri um** of the altar

a mā' bi lis, a mā' bi le lovable; **a mā bi' li a** lovable things

an' ge lus *m* angel **an' ge lī** of the angel

a' ni mal *n* animal **a ni mā' lis** of the animal

a' si na *f* donkey **a' si nae** of the donkey

bo' nus, bo' na, bo' num good; **bo' na** good things

ci' bus *m* food **ci' bī** of the food

cō' gi tō I think on **cō gi tā' re** to consider; **cō gi tā' te** (*imp*) think on!

cūr why

dē flec' tō I turn aside **dē flec' te re** to turn aside; **dē flec' tit** he, she, it turns aside

De' us *m* God **De' ī** of God

dī' cō I say, **dī' ce re** to say; **dī' cit** he, she, it, says

dō I give **da' re** to give; **dat** he, she, it gives

Do' mi nus *m* Lord **Do'mi nī** of the Lord

do' mus *f* home **do' mūs** of the home

e' dō I eat **e' de re** to eat; **e' dit** he, she, it eats

er' gō therefore

es you are; **est** he, she, it is

et and

fa' ci ō I make, I do **fa' ce re** to do, to make

fā'ma *f* report, reputation **fā' mae bo' nae** of good report, reputation

fī' li us *m* son **fī' li ī** of the son

haec these things

her' ba *f* grass **her' bae** of the grass

hi run' dō *f* swallow (a bird) **hi run' di nis** of the swallow

in in

in ve' ni ō I find **in ve nī' re** to find; **in' ven it** he, she, it finds

iūs' tus, iūs' ta, iūs' tum just; **iūs' ta** just things

le' ō *m* lion **le ō' nis** of the lion

lu' pus *m* wolf **lu' pī** of the wolf

ma' lus, ma' la, ma' lum bad, evil

mē me

me' us, me' a, me' um my, mine

mōns *m* mountain **mon' tis** of the mountain

nī' dus *m* nest **nī' dī** of the nest

nōn no, not

numquam never

oc cī' dō I kill **oc cī' de re** to kill; **oc cī' dit** he, she, it kills

par' ti ō I share **par tī' re** to share; **par' ti unt** they share

pas' ser *m* sparrow **pas' se ris** of the sparrow

pa' ter *m* father **pa' tris** of the father

pis' cis *m* fish **pis' cis** of the fish

por' tō I carry **portā' re** to carry; **por' tat** he, she, it carries

prophē' ta *m* prophet **pro phē' tae** of the prophet

pul' vis *m* dust **pul' ve ris** of the dust

pū' ni ō I punish **pū nī' re** to punish; **pū' nīs** you punish

pū' rus, pū' ra, pū' rum pure **pū' ra** pure things

quae (things) which

quae' rō I seek, I ask **quae' re re** to seek, to ask **quae' rit** he, she, it asks

qui' a because

rēx *m* king **rē' gis** of the king

sānc' tus, sānc' ta, sānc' tum holy **sānc' ta** holy things

sa' pi ēns *gen* **sa pi ent' is** wise

sī if

sum I am

tau' rus *m* bull **tau' rī** of the bull

tū, tē you

tu' us, tu' a, tu' um your, yours

vē' rus vē' ra vē' rum true; **vē' ra** true things

vi' a *f* road, path **vi' ae** of the road

vi' de ō I see; **vi dē' re** to see; **videt** he, she, it sees

vī' pe ra *f* snake **vī' pe rae** of the snake

vī' vō I live **vī' ve re** to live; **vī' vis** you live

vo' cō I call **vocā' re** to call; **vo' cat** he, she, it calls

SECTION II
Fēmina Bona

Adapted from Proverbs 31:10 & 25

Fēmina bona pretium magnum habet. Fortitūdō et honor
vestis eius sunt.

Adapted from Romans 16:6

Quamquam Christiānī Rōmae* sunt in perīculō, Marīa, fēmina
Christiāna in Rōmā, prō Paulō et Christiānīs multum labōrat.

Adapted from Romans 16:1–2

Phēbē, fēmina Graeca, Apostulō Paulō et aliīs Christiānīs
auxilium dat. Apostulus Paulus ex Graeciā Rōmānīs epistulam
scrībit. Phēbē Rōmānīs epistulam portat.

Anus Fidem Habet
Adapted from Acts and Timothy

Anus Lois in Lystrā cum fīliā Eunice habitat. Eunice fīlium
Timōtheum habet. Lois et Eunice Timōtheum Scrīptūram
docent. Timōtheus iuvenis cum Apostulō Paulō prō
Christiānīs labōrat.

Vocabulary for Section II

NB: Appendix III provides additional help with noun endings.

alius alia aliud other **aliīs** to others

anus anūs *f* old woman

apostulus apostulī *m* one sent with good news, apostle, missionary

auxilium auxiliī *n* help, aid

Christiānus Christiānī *m* follower of Christ, Christian

cum with

doceō docēre to teach *takes two direct objects*

eius his, hers, its

epistula epistulae *f* letter (*to someone*), epistle

ex from, out of

fēmina fēminae *f* woman

fidēs fideī *f* faith

fīlia fīliae *f* daughter

fortitūdō fortitūdinis *f* strength

Graecus Graeca Graecum Greek

Graecia Graeciae *f* Greece

habeō habēre to have

habitō habitāre to live, to dwell

honor honōris *m* honor

iuvenis iuvenis iuvene young; *m* young man

labōrō labōrāre to work

magnus magna magnum large, great

multus multa multum much

perīculum perīculī *n* danger

pretium pretiī *n* value, price

prō for

quamquam although

Rōma Rōmae *f* Rome; * **Rōmae** (*loc*) in Rome

Rōmānus Rōmāna Rōmānum Roman

scrībō scrībere to write

Scrīptūra Scrīptūrae *f* a writing, holy writing, scripture

sunt they are

vestis vestis *f* clothing, clothes

Section III
Vir Bonus

Adapted from Luke 6:43 & 45

Arbor bona nōn habet frūctum malum et arbor mala nōn habet frūctum bonum. Bonus vir in bonō corde habet bonum dum malus vir in malō corde habet malum.

Adapted from Luke 23:50–53

Iōsēphus ab Arimathaeā, vir bonus et iūstus, rēgnum Deī exspectat. Post mortem Iēsū, Iōsēphus ad Pilātum accēdit et corpus Iēsū petit. Corpus Iēsū in sepulchrō novō Iōsēphus pōnit.*

Adapted from Acts 11:22–24

Christiānī Ierosolymae ad Antiochiam Barnabas mittit quia apostulī Dominum Iēsum ad Graecōs ibi annūntiant. Barnabas, vir bonus, discipulōs novōs videt et laetus est.*

Adapted from Acts 11:28–30

Dum Barnabas et Apostulus Paulus in Antiochiā Ēvangelium annūntiat, Christiānī veniunt et fāmem magnam nārrant. Barnabas et Paulus ex Christiānīs in Antiochiā ad Ierosolymam pecūniam portant.[*]

---

[*] *This story is in the Latin historical present tense, which means that it can be put in or read as the past tense in English.*

Vocabulary for Section III

NB: *In this vocabulary we have added a new feature. Prepositions will now be marked as taking the accusative case or the ablative case after them. See Appendices III and IV for noun forms.*

Also, beginning with this vocabulary, verbs will be listed in the vocabulary with four principal parts. Some will not have four principal parts because they are defective—they lack one or more principal parts. Meanings and uses of the four principal parts are discussed in Appendix VII. Principal parts for verbs listed in Sections I, II, and III may be found in the glossary.

ab *prep w abl* from

accēdō accēdere accessī accessum to approach

ad *prep w acc* to

annūntiō annūntiāre annūntiāvī annūntiātum to proclaim, to announce

Antiochia Antiochiae *f* city of Antioch

arbor arboris *f* tree

Arimathaea Arimathaeae *f* the city of Arimathaea

Barnabas *indecl* Barnabas

cor cordis *n* heart

corpus corporis *n* body

discipulus discipulī *m* learner, pupil, disciple

dum *conj* while

Ēvangelium Ēvangeliī *n* Good News, Gospel

exspectō exspectāre exspectāvī exspectātum to await, to expect

famēs famis *f* hunger, famine

frūctus frūctūs *m* fruit

ibi *adv* there

Ierosolyma Ierosolymae *f* the city of Jerusalem

Iēsus Iēsū *m* Jesus

Iōsēphus Iōsēphī *m* Joseph

laetus laeta laetum happy, fortunate

magnus magna magnum large, great

mittō mittere mīsī missum to send

mors mortis *f* death

nārrō nārrāre nārrāvī nārrātum to tell, to tell about

novus nova novum new

pecūnia pecūniae *f* money

petō petere petīvī petītum to seek, ask

Pilātus Pilātī *m* Roman governor of Judea

pōnō pōnere posuī positum to put

post *prep w acc* after

rēgnum rēgnī *n* kingdom

sepulchrum sepulchrī *n* grave, tomb

veniō venīre vēnī ventum to come

vir virī *m* man

Section IV
Iuvenēs Bonī

Adapted from 1 Timothy 4:12

Sī exemplum fidēle in verbō, in conversātiōne, in cāritāte, in fidē, et in cāstitāte es, nēmō iuventam tuam contemnit.

Adapted from Zechariah 8:3 & 5

Dominus dīcit: "Sum in Sion, et habitō in mediā Ierosolymā et Ierosolyma erit cīvitās vēritātis, et mōns Dominī est mōns sānctus."
"Et viae cīvitātis erunt plēnae puerīs et puellīs in lūdō."

Samuēl Puer

Adapted from I Samuel 2:18 & 26 and I Samuel 3:19–20

Samuēl puer ministrat ante Dominum, accinctus ephod līneō. Et puer Samuēl crēscit. Placet et Dominō et virīs. Samuēl adolēscit, et Dominus est cum eō, et verba eius in terram nōn cadunt. Nunc omnis Israēl cognōscit: Samuēl est prophēta Dominī.

Dāvīd Iuvenis

Adapted from I Samuel 16:11–13, 18

Samuēl dīcit, "Isai, suntne hī omnēs līberī tuī?" Isai dīcit: "Est parvulus, quī cūrat ovēs." Samuēl dīcit, "Vocā eum," et Dāvīd venit. Nunc Dāvīd est rūfus et pulcher. Dominus dīcit, "Surge, unge eum; ūnus est." Samuēl Dāvīdem ungit, et Spīritus Dominī in Dāvīde est. Servus Rēgis Saūlis dīcit, "Dāvīd Bethlehemīticus psallit bene; est fortis in bellō et prūdēns in verbīs et pulcher est."

NB: *This story is in the Latin historical present, which means that it can be put in or read as the past tense in English.*

Vocabulary for Section IV

NB: In this section we have varied noun forms. Appendix V sheds light on these.

In this and subsequent vocabularies a bullet will indicate the end of the base word, and endings will be given which attach to it to form the other principal parts of the word. For example, the adjective "līne·us –a –um of linen" if written out in full would be "līneus, līnea, līneum of linen."

First conjugation verbs whose parts are regular will be marked as 1. Their parts all follow the pattern of "nārrō nārrāre nārrāvī nārrātum."

accinct·us –a –um girded, belted

adolēsc·ō –ere adolēvī adultum to grow up

ante *prep w acc* before

bell·um –ī *n* war

bene *adv* well

Bethlemītic·us –a –um pertaining to Bethelehem, of Bethelehem

cad·ō –ere cecidī cāsum to fall

cārit·ās –ātis *f* love, esteem

castit·ās –ātis *f* purity

cīvit·ās –ātis *f* city, state

cognōsc·ō –ere cognōvī cognitum to know

contemn·ō –ere contempsī contemptum to look down on, to condemn

conversāt·iō –iōnis *f* interaction

crēsc·ō –ere crēvī crētum to grow, to increase

cūrō 1 to take care of

Dāv·īd –īdis *m* David

eō *pron* by, with him

ephod *indecl* a Jewish vestment

erit he, she, it will be

erunt they will be

et ... et both ... and

exempl·um –ī *n* example

fīdel·īs –e faithful

fort·is –e brave, strong

hic haec hoc this; *n pl* haec these things

Iasi *indecl* Jesse

Israēl *indecl* Israel*

iuvent·a –ae *f* youth

līber·ī –ōrum *m pl* children

līne·us –a –um of linen

lūd·us –ī *m* play

medi·us –a –um middle of

ministr·ō 1 to serve, to minister to

nēm·ō –inis *m* no one, nobody

numquam *adv* never

nunc *adv* now

omn·is –e everyone, everything

ov·is –is *f* sheep

parv·us –a –um small, young; parvulus youngest

plac·eō –ēre –uī –itum *w dat* to please, to be pleasing to

plēn·us –a –um full, filled with

prūd·ēns *gen* –entis careful, discreet

psall·ō –ere –ī –– to play the harp

puell·a –ae *f* girl

puer puerī *m* boy

pul·cher –chra –chrum handsome, beautiful, good-looking

quī quae quod *pron* who, which

rūf·us –a –um red, ruddy, having a healthy complexion

Samuēl Samuēlis *m* Samuel*

Saul Saūlis *m* Saul

serv·us –ī *m* servant, slave

Sion *indecl* City of Zion, Jerusalem

spīrit·us –ūs *m* spirit

surg·ō –ere surrēxī surrēctum to rise

terr·a –ae *f* earth, ground

ung·ō –ere ūnxī ūnctum to anoint with oil

ūn·us –a –um one

verb·um –ī *n* word

vērit·ās –ātis *f* truth

---

* *Many names such as Israel and Samuel have been brought into Latin from other languages and do not lend themselves to Latin declension.*

SECTION V
Senēs

Adapted from Psalm 37:25

Iuvenis fuī, nunc senex sum; nec vīdī iūstum dēsertum, nec
līberōs suōs quaerentēs pānem.

Adapted from Psalm 71:9, 17–18

Nōlī prōicere mē in senectūte, ubi fortitūdō mea mē dēserit.
Deus, docuistī mē ā iuventā, et prōnūntiāvī operās tuās.
Nunc, in senectūte, Deus, nōlī mē dēserere; dēmōnstrābō
fortitūdinem tuam generātiōnī huic.

Ioshua, Vir Deī
Adapted from Exodus 17 & 24; Numbers 13–14

Ioshua fīlius Nun iuvenis Hebraeus in Aegyptō fuit. Moyses
Ioshuam ministrum suum fēcit. Ioshua et Hebraeī Amalek
victōriā magnā vīcērunt.

    Moyses et Ioshua minister eius in montem Deī ascendērunt.
Ioshua exspectāvit, et Moyses sōlus in nūbēs glōriae Deī
ascendit. Moyses verba Deī recēpit.

Moyses speculātōrēs in terram Chanaān mīsit. Ubi
revēnērunt, aliquī speculātōrēs dīxērunt, "Terra bona fluit
lacte et melle, sed virī terrae fortēs sunt." Sōlī Ioshua et Caleb
dīxērunt, "Terra bona fluit lacte et melle, et nostra erit."

Moyses senex erat; vocāvit Ioshuam, et prō ūniversō Israēl
eī dīxīt, "Dūc populum in terram quam Dominus dēdit."

Dominus Ioshuae dīxit, "Estō fortis; dūc in terram fīliōs
Israēl. Ego tēcum erō." Ioshua fīliōs Israēl in terram dūxit;
multōs victōriīs magnīs vīcit; terram inter fīliōs Israel dīvīsit.

Ioshua senex erat; vocāvit fīliōs Israēl et eīs dīxit, "Dedī
vōbīs terram in quā nōn labōrāvistis et urbēs quās nōn
aedificāvistis. Nunc timēte Dominō et servīte Eī. Sī hoc nōn
tibi bonum est, ēligite hodiē dominum. Ego et domus mea
Dominō serviēmus."

Fīliī Israēl respondērunt, "Dominus Deus noster nōs et
patrēs nostrōs dē terrā Aegyptō dūxit. Ēiēcit populōs terrae in
quā habitāmus. Ergō Dominō, quī est Deus noster, serviēmus."

Et post haec mortuus est Ioshua fīlius Nun, servus Dominī,
centum et decem annōs nātus.

Vocabulary for Section V

aedific·ō 1 to build

Aegypt·us –ī *f* Egypt

aliquis aliquid someone, something; *pl* some

Amalek *indecl* Amalekites, a nomadic tribe

ann·us –ī *m* year

ascend·ō –ere –ī ascēnsum to ascend

Caleb *indecl* an Israelite

centum *indecl* one hundred

Chanaān *indecl* Canaan

decem *indecl* ten

dēmōnstr·ō 1 to show, to demonstrate

dēser·ō –ere dēseruī dēsertum to desert, to abandon

dīvid·ō –ere dīvīsī dīvīsum to divide

dō dare dedī datum to give

dūc·ō –ere dūxī ductum to lead; **dūc** *imp* lead

dux ducis *m* leader

ego *pron* I

ē·iciō –icere –iēcī –iectum to throw out, to eject

ēlig·ō –ere ēlēgī ēlēctum to choose; **ēligite** *imp* choose

erat he, she, it was

erit he, she, it will be

erō I shall be

estō *imp* be

flu·ō –ere –xī –xum to flow

generāti·ō –ōnis *f* generation

habit·ō 1 to live

Hebrae·us –ī *m* Hebrew

hodiē *adv* today

huic to this

Ioshu·a –ae *m* Joshua

labōr·ō 1 to work

lac lactis *n* milk

mel mellis *n* honey

minis·ter –trī *m* attendant, helper, minister

mortuus est he died

Moyses *indecl* Moses

nāt·us –a –um born

nec *adv* not; **nec . . . nec** neither . . . nor

nōlō nōlle to be unwilling, to not want; **nōlī** *w infin* don't

nōs *pron* we, us

nost·er –ra –rum our

nūb·ēs –is *f* cloud

Nun *indecl* Nun

oper·a –ae *f* work

pān·is –is *m* bread

popul·us –ī *m* tribe or people

prō·iciō –icere –iēcī –iectum to cast away, to throw forth

prōnūnti·ō 1 to proclaim

quā *pron* by whom, by which

quam *pron* whom, which

quās *pron f pl* whom, which

recip·iō –ere recēpī receptum to receive

respond·eō –ēre respondī respōnsum to respond

reven·iō –īre revēnī reventum to return

sed *conj* but

senect·ūs –ūtis *f* old age

senex senis *m* old man

serv·iō –īre servīvī servītum *dat obj* to serve; **servīte** *imp* serve

sōl·us –a –um alone, only

speculātor speculātōris *m* spy

super *prep w acc* above

tibi *pron* to, for you

tim·eō –ēre –uī –– to fear, to be afraid; **timēte** *imp* fear

ubi *conj* when, where

ūnivers·us –a –um all, whole, entire

urb·s –is *f* city

victōri·a –ae *f* victory

vinc·ō –ere vīcī victum to conquer

vōbīs to, for, by, with you *pl*

SECTION VI
Mātrēs et Līberī

Adapted from Ezekiel 19:10

Māter tua est vīneae similis in sanguine tuō, crēscentī iūxtā aquās multās.

Māter Samuelis

Adapted from Samuel 1 & 2

Elcana, servus Dominī Deī, uxōrem Annam amāvit. Anna līberōs nōn habuit. Anna dīxit, "Domine Deus, dā mihi fīlium, et eum tibi, Dominō, dabō."

Samuēl fīlius Elcanae et Annae nātus, ministrat ante Dominum, accinctus ephod līneō. Omnī annō Samuēl crēvit, et māter Samuēlis tunicam parvam novam fīliō fēcit.

Māter Moyses

Adapted from Exodus 1 & 2

Pharao, Rēx Aegyptī, vīdit fīliōs Israēl esse multōs. "Puerōs
nātōs Īsrāēlīticōs occīdite statim," dīxit. Māter īnfantis
Moyses fīlium trēs mēnsēs cēlāvit. Puer crēvit; cēlāre eum
nōn possibile erat. Māter īnfantem Moyses in fiscellā posuit.
Fiscellam in cārectō in rīpā flūminis posuit. Soror Moyses
procul fiscellam spectāvit. Fīlia Pharao fiscellam et īnfantem
invēnit. "Hic," fīlia Pharao dīxit, "est īnfāns Hebraeōrum."
Soror Moyses dīxit, "Sī vīs, vocābō fēminam Hebraeam quae
eum cūrābit." Ergō māter Moyses eum cūrāvit, et fīlia Pharao
eum fīlium vōcāvit.

Cornēlia, Māter Gracchōrum (c. 210 BC–c. 160 BC)
Ancient history only sparsely records the contributions of women. An
exception is Cornelia, the learned and gifted daughter of Scipio Africanus. She
was the wife and daughter of outstanding patriots; she bore twelve children
of whom only three survived into adulthood. She said in her adult years that
she hoped to be now known, not just as the daughter of Africanus, but as the
mother of the Gracchi. Her own temperate and intelligent advice helped her
sons during their brief lives and served her country long after their deaths.

The story of the jewels is told by Valerius Maximus. Possibly he drew from
Livy's *Ab Urbe Conditā*. Livy, of course, must then have been following some
earlier source. The Roman writer Quintilian in *Īnstitūtiōnēs Orātōriae*, 1.1 says
that Cornelia helped train her boys for oratory, as speechmaking was a very
important skill for leading politicians in the Roman Republic.

Two extracts from letters of Cornelia are preserved in manuscripts of
Cornelius Nepos, which letters many regard as genuine. If so, they are perhaps
the earliest letters by a Roman woman extant. They certainly make interesting
reading. There exists, too, the base of a statue, found in the 1870s at Rome,
inscribed simply *CORNELIA AFRICANI F. / GRACCHORUM* (understand
"mater") in Augustan age lettering. On it may have stood the statue mentioned
by Pliny in his *Nātūrālis Historia* 34.31, and Plutarch in C. *Gracchus* 4.

Adapted from Valerius Maximus, *Factōrum et Dictōrum Memorābilium Librī Novem* 4.4.1 and Quīntiliānus, *Īnstitūtiōnēs Orātōriae* 1.1

Tiberius Semprōnius Gracchus, marītus Cornēliae secundae fīliae Scipiōnis Āfricānī, dux Rōmānōrum, vir honestātis erat. Hispānī, quōs aequē rēxit, praecipuē eum in memoriā cārā tenuērunt. Cornēlia erat multō iūnior quam marītus Semprōnius Gracchus. Post mortem Gracchī, māter sōla suōs fīliōs duōs Tiberium et Gāium ēducāvit. Cornēlia, docta et intellegēns fēmina cuius epistulae ēloquentēs erant, līberōs suōs multa dē eōrum gente et patriā docuit.

Scrīptor Rōmānus Quīntiliānus dīxit, "Disciplīna Cornēliae ōrātiōnēs fīliōrum eius firmāvit." Sīcut aliī gentis suae, Cornēlia nōn luxuriam sed patriam amāvit. Fēminae ostendentī gemmās suās, Cornēlia suōs fīliōs mōnstrāvit. "Hī," dīxit, "sunt gemmae meae."

Vocabulary for Section VI

aequ·us –a –um just; aequē justly

cār·us –a –um dear

cārect·um –ī n a bed of reeds

cēl·ō 1 to conceal

disciplīn·a –ae f teaching, education

du·o –ae –o two

ēduc·ō 1 to bring up, to raise

ēloquēns gen ēloquentis eloquent, well expressed

firm·ō 1 to strengthen

fiscell·a –ae f small basket

flūm·en –inis n river

gemm·a –ae f jewel

gēns gentis f clan, family, tribe, people, nation

Hispān·us –ī m Spaniard

honest·ās –ātis f integrity

in memoriā tenēre to remember

intelligēns gen intellegentis intelligent, understanding

iūni·or –us younger

iūxtā adv near, beside

luxuri·a –ae f luxury

marīt·us –ī m husband

mēns·is mēnsis m month

mōnstr·ō 1 to show

nov·us –a –um new

ōrāti·ō –ōnis f speech, manner of speaking, eloquence

ostendō ostendere ostendī ostentum to show; ostendentī showing (see Appendix VII)

patri·a –ae f fatherland, country

Pharao m indecl Pharoah, rulers of Egypt

possibil·is –e possible

praecipu·us –a –um special, particular; praecipuē especially

procul adv far off, at a distance

quam in comparisons than

reg·ō –ere rēxī rēctum to rule

rīp·a –ae f riverbank

sangui·s –nis m blood, race

scrīpt·or –ōris m writer

secund·us –a –um second, following, next

sīcut conj just like

simil·is –e similar, like

sor·or –ōris f sister

spect·ō 1 to watch, to look at

statim adv at once, immediately

su·us –a –um his own, her own, its own

trēs tria three

tunic·a –ae f tunic, coat, garment

ux·or –ōris f wife

vīne·a –ae f vine

volō velle voluī to want, to wish; vīs you wish, you want

Section VII
Patrēs et Līberī

Adapted from Proverbs 13:1

Fīlius sapiēns disciplīnam patris audit.

Adapted from Proverbs 23:26

Dā mihi cor tuum, fīlī mī, et spectā viās meās.

Fīlius Prōdigus

Adapted from Luke 15:11–24

Vir quīdam duōs fīliōs habuit, et iūnior patrī dīxit, "Pater, dā mihi portiōnem substantiae quae mea erit."

Pater substantiam dīvīsit et mox iūnior fīlius in terram longinquam vēnit. Ibi substantiam cōnsūmpsit vīvendō in luxuriā. Postquam substantiam cōnsūmpsit, iēiūnus erat, et porcōs virī cūrāvit. Siliquās, cibum porcōrum, edere voluit. Dīxit, "Servī patris meī cibum multum habent, et ego iēiūnus sum. Vādam ad patrem meum."

Vēnit ad patrem suum et dīxit, "Pater, peccāvī, et nōn sum dignus vocārī fīlius tuus. Erō servus tuus." Pater servīs dīxit, "Dāte vestēs optimās fīliō meō quī mortuus erat, sed quī nunc vīvit. Parāte epulum eī."

Cato Censor (234 BC–149 BC)

Cato was born a plebeian or commoner. He fought well as a military tribune in the Second Punic War; then, even though rising in the political world was usually achieved only by the patricians, or aristocratic Romans, he began the course of honors, or elected offices which led to political power in the Roman Republic. As consul he refined Roman power in Spain. At Thermopylae Cato fought against the Syrians and overcame the enemies of Rome. In war he marched alongside his soldiers; he took no loot. His life was an example of economy; he had enough money to live simply and did not desire more. Cato worked alongside his slaves and consumed simple food and wine with them. As proconsul in Sardinia, despising the carriages and guesthouses provided at the expense of provincials, he advanced on foot with one slave.

As censor Cato corrected many evils. He imposed a large tax upon citizens for luxury; he cut off the public water flowing into private buildings; private buildings built on public property were destroyed.

Often he pled the causes of oppressed provincials. When the consul Servius Sulpicius Galba killed many Lusitanians who had been led to surrender by words of peace, Cato in his ninetieth year brought him to trial in Rome.

The Roman writer Livy (*Ab Urbe Condita* 5.39–40) said of Cato: "He was severe in mind and harsh in language, but unconquered by the desires of the human spirit, unyielding in his integrity, contemptuous of influence and of riches. No skill for getting things done either public or private was lacking in him; he was equally able in affairs of city or countryside. Knowledge of the law advances some to the highest offices; eloquence, others; military glory, others: his natural ability for all things was so equally adapted to all things that whatever he was doing, you might say he was born to do that one thing."

Catō Liciniānus, Discipulus Patrī, Catonis Censoris

Adapted from Livy, *Ab Urbe Condita* 5.39

Marcus Porcius Catō, ex familiā Rōmānā paupere nātus, in agrō parvō labōrāvit. Quamquam vir Catō cōnsul cēnsorque erat, vītam simplicem amat. Rōmānī victōriās magnās et divītiās magnās habuērunt, sed luxuriam et divītiās Catō improbāvit. Quamquam Catō multa negōtia habuit, tamen fīlium suum, Catōnem Liciniānum, dīligenter dē vītā simplicī ēducāvit. Prīmum librum dē historiā, deinde librōs dē agricultūrā et medicīnā et mōribus pater Catō scrīpsit; ex eīs librīs fīlium docuit. Catō erat vir sevērus, sed uxōrī et fīliō benignus erat. "Nocēre uxōrī aut līberīs," dīxit, "est nocēre sacerrimīs." Quod Catō Liciniānus vir honestātis erat, gaudiō patrī suō erat. Licinia, māter Catōnis Liciniānī, mortua est, et uxōrem secundam Catō in mātrimōnium dūxit. Fīliō suō dīxit, "Uxōrem secundam dūxī, quod cupiō fīliōs aliōs similēs tuī."

Vocabulary for Section VII

ag·er –rī *m* field

agricultūr·a –ae *f* agriculture, farming

aud·iō –īre –īvī –ītum to hear

aut *conj* or; **aut . . . aut** either . . . or

benign·us –a –um kind

Catō Catōnis *m* Cato

cēns·or –ōris *m* censor *(one of two officials elected every five years to take census and censure morals)*

cōnsul cōnsulis *m* consul *(one of the two highest elected officials in Rome; elected annually)*

cōnsūm·ō –ere cōnsūmpsī cōnsūmptum to use up, to waste

cor cordis *n* heart

cup·iō –ere cupīvī cupītum to want, to desire

deinde *adv* then

dign·us –a –um worthy

dīligēns *gen* **dīligentis** industrious, diligent; **dīligenter** diligently

divīti·ae –ārum *f pl* riches

epul·um –ī *n* banquet

famili·a –ae *f* family, household

gaud·ium –ī *n* joy, gladness

hab·eō –ēre –uī –itum to have

histori·a –ae *f* history

iēiūn·us –a –um hungry, fasting

improb·ō 1 disapprove of, condemn

in mātrimōnium dūcere to lead (a woman) into marriage, to marry

li·ber –brī *m* book

longinqu·us –a –um far off, distant

medicīn·a –ae *f* medicine

mōs moris *m* custom, habit, usual standard of behavior

mox *adv* soon

negōt·ium –ī *n* business

noc·eō –ēre nocuī nocitum to injure, to harm

optim·us –a –um best

par·ō 1 to prepare

paup·er –era –erum poor

pecc·ō 1 to sin

porc·us –ī *m* hog, pig

porti·ō –ōnis *f* share

postquam *conj* after, when

prīmum *adv* first, in the beginning, at first

–que *(syllable added at the end of a word to link it with the previous word)* and

quīdam quaedam quiddam a certain person, a certain thing

quod *conj* because

sac·er –ra –rum sacred, holy; **sacerrimus** most sacred

sevēr·us –a –um strict, severe

siliqu·a –ae *f* husk

simplex *gen* **simplicis** simple, plain

spect·ō 1 to observe, to watch, to look at

substanti·a –ae *f* wealth, property

tamen *adv* yet, nevertheless

vād·ō –ere vāsī – – to go

victōri·a –ae *f* victory

vīt·a –ae *f* life

Section VIII
Amīcī

Adapted from Proverbs 17:17

Amīcus tuus omnī tempore tē dīligit.

Adapted from John 15:13

Est nōn māior dīlēctiō quam haec: amīcus prō amīcīs suīs animam suam dēpōnit.

Adapted from John 21:15

Iēsus Simōnī Petrō dīxit, "Dīligisne mē?" Dīxit Petrus, "Domine, tū scīs mē tē amāre."*

David and Jonathan
Adapted from 1 Samuel 18, 23, 31; 2 Samuel 4, 9

Rēx Saūl iuvenem Dāvīdem in domum suam recēpit, et Dāvīd ibi habitāvit. Iōnathan, fīlius rēgis, Dāvīdem dīlēxit sīcut animam suam et eī arma et vestēs suās dēdit. Dāvīd omnia quae Saūl rogāvit dīligenter fēcit, et Saūl eum belligerīs praefēcit.

---

* *Jesus used "dīligis," an intense word for love that indicates "I love you more than anyone." Peter used "amō," which is a more ordinary word for loving in various ways.*

Michol, fīlia Rēgis Saūlis, Dāvīdem amāvit, et Dāvīd eam
amāvit et in mātrimōnium dūxit. Sed Saūl iuvenem Dāvīdem
timēre coepit, et eum nōn amāvit. Saūl eum occīdere voluit, sed
Michol et Iōnathan eum servāvērunt.

Identidem Saūl iuvenem Dāvīdem occīdere temptāvit.
Iōnathan fīlius Saūlis ad Dāvīdem in silvam vēnit et dīxit,
"Saūl, pater meus, tē nōn inveniet. Tū Israēl regēs, et erō tibi
secundus." Ergō Iōnathan et Dāvīd foedus cōram Dominō
īcērunt.

Philisthīnī cum Israēl pugnāvērunt. Philisthīni Saūlem et
Iōnathan et aliōs fīliōs Saūlis occīdērunt. Iōnathan fīlius Saūlis
fīlium Miphibosheth quīnque annōs nātum habuit. Quandō
nūntius dē morte Saūlis et Iōnathan vēnit, nūtrīx puerī portāns
puerum fūgit. Nūtrīx cecidit, et puer claudus factus est.

Dāvīd omnem Israēl rēxit. Dāvīd dīxit, "Superestne aliquis
dē domō Saūlis cui misericordiam mōnstrem prō Iōnathan?"
Siba servus dīxit, "Fīlius amīcī tuī Iōnathan vīvit. Claudus
est." "Ubi est?" Dāvīd rogāvit. Rēx Dāvīd Miphibosheth, fīlium
Iōnathan, ad domum suam vocāvit. Quandō Miphibosheth
vēnit, Dāvīd dīxit, "Tibi omnēs agrōs Saūlis dō, et apud
mēnsam meam semper edēs." Miphibosheth dīxit, "Servus
tuus sum, sed cūr honōrem mihi dās?"

Dāvīd dīxit, "Prō Iōnathan, quem dīlēxī sīcut animam
meam."

Vocabulary for Section VIII

ali·quis –quid someone, anyone, something

amīc·us –ī *m* friend

anim·a –ae *f* life, soul

apud *prep w acc* at

arm·a –ōrum *n pl* weapons, arms

belliger·us –ī *m* man of war

cad·ō –ere cecidī cāsum to fall

claud·us –a –um lame, crippled

coep·ī –isse –tus *def* to begin

cōram *prep w abl* in the presence of, before

cui to whom

dē·pōnō –pōnere –posuī –positum to put down, to lay down

dīlēcti·ō –ōnis *f* love (Late Latin)

dīlig·ō –ere dīlēxī dīlēctum to love above all others

edēs you will eat (*see Appendix VIII*)

foed·us –eris *n* agreement, pact, treaty; **foedus īcere** to make a pact or treaty

fug·iō –ere fūgī fugitum to run away, to flee

identidem *adv* again and again

inveniet he will find (*see Appendix VIII*)

māior māius greater

mēns·a –ae *f* table

misericordi·a –ae *f* kindness, pity, mercy

nūnti·us –ī *m* messenger, message

nūtrīx nūtrīcis *f* nurse

Pet·rus –rī *m* Peter

Philisthīn·us –ī *m* Philistine

pugn·ō 1 to fight

quandō *conj* when

quīnque *indecl* five

rog·ō 1 to ask

sc·iō –īre –īvī –ītum to know

semper *adv* always

serv·ō 1 to save, to preserve

silv·a –ae *f* forest

Sim·ōn –ōnis *m* Simon

super·sum –esse –fuī –futūrus to be left over, to survive

suprā *prep w acc* over, above

temp·us –oris *n* time

tempt·ō 1 to try, to attempt

Section IX
Amīcī Hominum

Adapted from Matthew 25:40

Quandō cūrās hōs frātrēs meōs, cūrās mē.

Adapted from 2 Peter 1:7

Ministrāte in pietāte amōrem frāternum, et in amōre frāternō
cāritātem.

Adapted from Acts 27:41–28:2

In nāvigātiōne Rōmam Rōmānī et captīvī, Paulō haud exceptō,
naufragium fēcērunt. Mīlitēs dīxērunt, "Occīdite captīvōs;
fugient!" Centuriō hoc vetuit et omnēs ad terram natāvērunt.

Erant in īnsulā Melitā. Barbarī misericordiam magnam
mōnstrāvērunt. Ignem fēcērunt; cibum ac refugium ex imbre
et frīgore omnibus dēdērunt.

Samarītānus Bonus

Adapted from Luke 10:30–37

Vir quī dēscendit ab Ierosolymā in Iericho ā latrōnibus
oppugnātus est. Latrōnēs eum spoliāvit et ferē mortuus relictus
est.* Sacerdōs hāc viā dēscendit; virum vīdit et praeterīvit.
Lēvīta hāc viā dēscendit; etiam virum vīdit et praeterīvit.

Deinde quīdam Samarītānus vēnit, et misericordiam eī
habuit. Vulnera cūrāvit, et virum posuit in suam asinam quam
in stabulum dūxit. Stabulāriō dīxit, "Hīc sunt duo dēnāriī.
Cūrā virum, et quandō reveniam, dēbitum quidquid tibi prō eō
dabō."

Iēsus dīxit, "Vāde, et fac similiter."

Nīcolāus dē Myrā (c. 270 AD to c. 345 AD)

Adapted from Symeon Metaphrastes, *Stories of Christianity*

Nīcolāus dē Myrā erat Epīscopus Ecclēsiae Christiānae urbis
Myrae in Āsiā Minōre. Persecūtiōnem Rōmānī Imperātōris
Dioclētiānī Nīcolāus tulit. Quandō Cōnstantīnus factus
est* prīmus Christiānus Imperātor Rōmānōrum, Nīcolāus
līberātus est* et iterum Christiānōs in Myrā cūrāvit. Mortuus
est sextō diē Decembris.

Nīcolāus hominēs dīlēxit. Praecipuē līberōs amāvit.
Fābulae dē eō multae sunt. Dīvītiās dē patre habuit, et dōna,
praecipuē in nātālī Iēsū, līberīs dedit. Post mortem Nīcolāī,
hominēs dōna dedērunt in nātālī Iesū et dīxērunt, "Sunt dōna
Sānctī Nīcolāī."

In multās terrās fābulae Sānctī Nīcolāī portātae sunt.*
Fōrmae nōminis eius sunt "Sinterklaus" et "Santa Claus."

---

* *See Appendix IX.*

Vocabulary for Section IX

ac *conj* as well as, and also

am·or –ōris *m* love

barbar·us –ī *m* barbarian, foreigner

captīv·us –ī *m* captive, prisoner

cārit·ās –ātis *f* generous love

centuri·ō –ōnis *m* Roman commander of one hundred soldiers

Cōnstantīn·us –ī *m* Constantine, Roman commander and emperor

dēb·eō –ēre dēbuī dēbitum to owe

Decem·ber –bris *m* December

dēnāri·us –ī *m* small coin, daily wage of a laborer in the first century AD

dēscend·ō –ere –ī dēscēnsum to go down, to descend

di·ēs –ēī *m* day

dōn·um –ī *n* gift

dūc·ō –ere –xī –ctum to lead

du·o –ae –o two

ecclēsi·a –ae *f* church

epīscop·us –ī *m* bishop

etiam *adv* also

fābul·a –ae *f* story

ferē *adv* almost

ferō ferre tulī lātum to bear, to endure, to carry

fōrm·a –ae *f* form, shape, likeness, beauty

frā·ter –tris *m* brother

frātern·us –a –um brotherly

frīg·us –oris *n* cold

haud exceptō *id* included; *lit* by no means left out

hīc *adv* here

hom·ō –inis *m* human being, man; *pl* people

Iericho *indecl* Jericho

ign·is –is *m* fire

imb·er –ris *m* rain

imperāt·or –ōris *m* commander, emperor

īnsul·a –ae *f* island

iterum *adv* again

latr·ō –ōnis *m* robber

Lēvīt·a –ae *m* Levite

līber·ō 1 to set free

Melit·a –ae *f* island of Malta

mīl·es –itis *m* soldier

nātāl·is –is *m* birthday

nat·ō 1 to swim

naufragi·um –ī *n* shipwreck; **naufragium facere** to be shipwrecked

nāvigāti·ō –ōnis *f* sea voyage

Nīcolā·us –ī *m* Nicholas

nōm·en –inis *n* name

oppugn·ō 1 to attack

persecūti·ō –ōnis *f* persecution

piet·ās –ātis *f* virtue, godliness

praeter·eō –īre –īvī –itum to pass by

prīm·us –a –um first

quisquis quidquid *pron* whoever, whatever

refug·ium –ī *n* refuge

relinqu·ō –ere relīquī relictum to leave, to leave behind, to abandon

sacerd·ōs –ōtis *m* priest

Sānctus Nīcolāus, Sānctī Nīcolāī *m* Saint Nicholas

sext·us –a –um sixth

similiter *adv* likewise, similarly

spoli·ō 1 to rob

stabulāri·us –ī *m* manager of a stable or lodging

stabul·um –ī *n* stable, sometimes with simple lodging

tulit see **ferō**

vād·ō –ere vāsī –– to go

vet·ō –āre –uī –itum to forbid

vuln·us –eris *n* wound, injury

SECTION X
Dominī

Adapted from Colossians 4:1

> Dominī, date quidquid servīs vestrīs est iūstum et aequum,
> quod vōs etiam Dominum in caelō habētis.

Gaius Plinius Caecilius Secundus (c. 61 AD–c. 113 AD)

Better known as Pliny the Younger, Pliny was a Roman patrician, or aristocrat. He was adopted by his maternal uncle Pliny the Elder, the admiral of the Roman fleet. He was a friend of the great historian Tacitus and of the Roman Emperor Trajan.

Pliny believed in and practiced the highest ideals of the Romans, and he took his responsibilities as head of household just as seriously as the duties occasionally assigned him by the Roman Emperor. The *paterfamilias* of a wealthy and noble house was responsible not only for his extended collection of relatives, but also for the *clientes, liberti,* servants, and slaves of his household. The patron and client system of Rome went back to the earliest days of the city. Roman patricians, or *patrones,* provided protection and assistance to lower class citizens in return for their loyalty; these became *clientes.* The clients in turn would help their patrons with whatever services they were able to render. A slave who had either earned or been given his freedom became a *libertus* and a client of his former master in addition to the Roman clients the patron might already have. The man who agreed to take care of the farm that Pliny had given to his old nurse was no doubt a client.

Pliny believed in good manners as part of the kindly treatment of people who belonged to all social classes. In Book 2, Letter 16, he is indignant because he has attended a banquet at which he and the other noble guests received choice food, "second class" guests received moderate food, and "lower class" guests received cheap food. He says that he invites his guests to enjoy themselves, not to be insulted, and that everyone at his table has the same food. When asked if such a policy would not become expensive, he said, "Not at all. We don't all eat the rich man's food; we all eat the poor man's food."

Adapted from Gaius Plinius Secundus, *Epistulae* 5:19

Videō molliter tē tuōs servōs habēre sīcut meōs tractō. Semper in animō meō est hoc verbum nostrum 'paterfamiliās.'

Adapted from Matthew 8:5–11, 13

Centuriō ad Iēsum vēnit et dīxit, "Domine, servus meus in domō paralyticus est, et male torquētur." Iēsus dīxit, "Vādam, et cūrābō eum." Centuriō dīxit, "Domine, nōn sum hospes dignus tē. Dīc verbum tantum, et servus meus cūrābitur. Namque sum homō quī potestātem habet. Mīlitēs mēcum habeō, et dīcō huic 'Vāde,' et vādit; et aliō, 'Venī' et venit; et servō meō 'Fac hōc,' et facit."

Iēsus discipulīs dīxit, "Nōn invēnī tantam fidem in Israēl. Dīcō vōbis, 'Multī ab oriente et ab occidente venient, et recumbent cum Abraham, Isaac, et Iacob in rēgnō caelī.'"

Iēsus centuriōnī dīxit, "Vāde, et sīcut crēdidistī, fiet tibi." Servus eius in illā hōrā cūrātus est.

Adapted from Gaius Plinius Secundus, *Epistulae* 6:3

Grātiās tibi agō quod agellum quem nūtrīcī meae dedī cūrābis. Pretium huius agellī erat centum mīlium nummōrum; nūper pretium dēcrēvit, sed nunc in manibus tuīs incrēscet.

Tibi committō nōn sōlum terram et arborēs, sed etiam dōnum meum. Quī dedit, sīcut quae recēpit, intentē cupit agellum esse quam frūctuōsissimum.

Vocabulary for Section X

aequ·us –a –um equal, fair

agell·um –ī *n* little field, little farm

arbor arboris *f* tree

cael·um –ī *n* heaven, sky

centum mīlium *n* one hundred thousand

centuri·ō –ōnis *m* Roman commander of one hundred soldiers, centurion

committ·ō –ere commīsī committum to entrust

crēd·ō –ere crēdidī crēditum to believe

cūrābitur he will be healed

dēcrēsc·ō –ere dēcrēvī dēcrētum to decrease

dign·us –a –um *w abl* worthy (of)

esse to be

fiet it shall be done

fid·ēs –ēī *f* faith

grātiās tibi agō I thank you

hōr·a –ae *f* hour

hosp·es –itis *m* host, guest

ill·e –a –ud that, that one

incrēsc·ō –ere incrēvī –– to grow, to increase

intentē *adv* earnestly, eagerly

man·us –ūs *f* hand

molliter *adv* gently

namque *conj* for

nōn sōlum . . . sed etiam *conj* not only . . . but also

numm·us –ī *m* coin (in this case, the sesterce)*

nūper *adv* recently

occid·ēns –entis *m* the west

ori·ēns –entis *m* the east

paralytic·us –a –um paralyzed

paterfamiliās patrisfamiliās *m* head of the household; *lit* father of the family

potest·ās –ātis *f* power

preti·um –ī *n* value, price

quam frūctuōsissimum as fruitful as possible

recip·iō –ere recēpī receptum to receive

recumb·ō –ere recubuī –– to recline at table with, to dine with

tantum *adv* only

torquētur he is tortured

tract·ō 1 to handle, to treat

vād·ō –ere vāsī –– to go

vest·er –ra –rum your *pl*

vōs *pron* you *pl*

---

* *Monetary value is extremely difficult to transfer from society to society, but, if the "nummus" in question is the usual sesterce, the original value of the farm would be around $25,000.*

SECTION XI
Magistrī et Discipulī

Adapted from Exodus 24:12

Dominus dīxit, "Moyses, venī ad montem, et dabō tibi lēgem et mandāta quae scrīpsī; et eōs docēbis."

Adapted from Matthew 11:1

Postquam Iēsus duodecim discipulōs docuit, vēnit ad urbēs et docuit.

Adapted from 2 Timothy 2:24

Servus Dominī est patiēns et mollis cum hominibus; docet modestiā.

Adapted from Titus 2:3

Anūs dignae magistrae sunt bonae; docent iuvenēs fēminās amōrem familiae.

Cyril (c. 826–869) and Methodius (c. 826–885)

These brothers were born into an aristocratic family of the Eastern Roman Empire centered in Constantinople. Their father, a military commander in Thessalonica, died when they were very young, and they were educated in Constantinople under the care of a powerful uncle. They entered a monastery, from which they were called to be Christian teachers in lands where their linguistic talents in Arabic, Hebrew, and the Slavonic tongue were needed. When the King of Moravia (Moravia is in the present day Czech Republic) requested Christian teachers who could conduct the Christian services in the Slavonic language, Cyril and Methodius were sent to him. Cyril invented an alphabet for the language of the Slavs, and he and Methodius translated the Gospels and other religious material into that language. They were called to Rome because some of the German churchmen questioned their use of the Slavonic language for church services. They were confirmed in their mission, but Cyril died in Rome in 869.

At the request of the princes of Moravia and Pannonia the churches of Moravia and Pannonia were made separate from the German churches and allowed to worship in the Slavic language. Methodius then went to Constantinople, where, with the assistance of several church scholars, he translated the whole Bible into the Slavic language. He served for some years as Archbishop of Moravia. He died in 885, naming Gorazd, a Moravian Slav who was his disciple, as his successor.

Cyril's alphabet, first called the Glagolitic, matched the specific features of the Slavic language. The alphabet which descended from it is called the Cyrillic, and is in use in many countries today.

А а	Б б	В в	Г г	Д д	Ђ ђ
Е е	Ж ж	З з	И и	Ј ј	К к
Л л	Љ љ	М м	Н н	Њ њ	О о
П п	Р р	С с	Т т	Ћ ћ	У у
Ф ф	Х х	Ц ц	Ч ч	Џ џ	Ш ш

Adapted from Ladislas Abraham, *Saints Cyril and Methodius*

Cyrillus et Methodius frātrēs erant quī nātī sunt in
Thessalonīcā. Pater eōrum, dux mīlitum, mortuus est, et
avunculus puerōs apud Cōnstantīnopolem ēducāvit. Diāconī
factī sunt, et quandō Rēx Moraviae apostolōs petīvit, Cyrillus
et Methodius Moraviam vēnērunt. Rēx Moraviae Evangelium
in linguā gēntis eius cupīvit. Cyrillus elementa in linguā
Moraviānōrum fēcit et in elementīs novīs Evangelium et
librōs Christiānōs scrīpsit. Methodius epīscopus Moraviae et
Pannoniae factus est postquam Cyrillus mortuus est. Hodiē
multae gentēs elementīs Cyrillī ūtuntur.

Marcus Fabius Quintilianus (c. 35 AD–c. 100 AD)

Marcus Fabius Quintilianus was born in Spain and evidently educated in
Rome. Around 69 this foremost of all Roman schoolmasters was launched
by the emperor on a career of teaching with an imperial subsidy. He taught
the children of the great, from Pliny the Younger to the grandnephews of the
Emperor Domitian, and seems to have been respected by men of letters such
as Tacitus and Juvenal. The poet Martial, not mincing matters, calls him "the
finest guide of Roman youth and the glory of the Roman toga" in a wistful little
poem about the happy life (*Epigrams* 2.90).

Quintilian's one extant work, the *Īnstitūtiōnēs Ōrātōriae*, is one of the
most sensitive, thorough, and positive works ever written on the education
of the young. It discusses methods of building character and of embracing
the liberal arts to produce a worthy citizen. The emperor Vespasian, a rough-
edged pragmatist who rose through the ranks of the military to power, made
Quintilian a consul. This emperor was no lover of the arts, but he believed good
education was the best means of molding intelligent and responsible citizens.

Adapted from Quintilian, *Īnstitūtiōnēs Ōrātōriae* 2.2

Prīmum, bonus magister scholae in memoriā tenet sē intrāre
locum parentēs quī līberōs eī commīsērunt. Ergō vitia nec
habet nec fert. Multa dē rēbus honestīs et bonīs dīcit: saepe
discipulōs mōnet, rārō castīgat. Perrārō est īrācundus; sī
tamen errant, nōn neglegit errōrēs. Bonōs discipulōs laudat;
in laudibus tamen nec malignus nec effūsus est. Namque

discipulī, sī semper laudās, mox labōribus sunt dēfessī; sī numquam, omnem labōrem neglegunt. Ubi ea ēmendat quae discipulī nōn satis bene aut dīxērunt aut scrīpsērunt, nōn est acerbus aut contumēliōsus. Magistrī nōn numquam ā studiīs discipulōs āvertunt quod acerbē eōs castīgant. Bonus magister cōtīdiē dīcit digna quae discipulī memoriā tenent. Namque magistrī officium est docēre, et discipulōrum discere.

Vocabulary for Section XI

acer·bus –a –um harsh, bitter; **acerbē** harshly

āvert·ō –ere –tī āversum to turn away

avuncul·us –ī *m* uncle

castīg·ō 1 to reprove, to scold

contumēliōs·us –a –um insulting

cōtīdiē *adv* daily

Cyrill·us –ī *m* Cyril, Apostle to the Slavs

dēfess·us –a –um tired, weary

diācon·us –ī *m* minister, servant of the church, deacon

**disc·ō –ere didicī –– ** to learn

duodecim *indecl* twelve

ēduc·ō 1 to bring up, to raise

effūs·us –a –um immoderate

element·a –ōrum *n pl* alphabet

ēmend·ō 1 to correct

err·ō 1 to make a mistake, to wander

error errōris *m* mistake

honest·us –a –um honorable, respected

intr·ō 1 to enter

īrācund·us –a –um angry

laud·ō 1 to praise

lau·s –dis *f* praise

lēx lēgis *f* law

lingu·a –ae *f* language, tongue

loc·us –ī *m* place

malign·us –a –um stingy, malicious

mandāt·um –ī *n* command, commandment

Methodi·us –ī *m* Methodius, brother of Cyril and Apostle to the Slavs

modesti·a –ae *f* restraint, discretion

moll·is –e gentle

mōn·eō –ēre –uī –itum to advise, to warn

Moravi·a –ae *f* Moravia, region in Central Europe roughly corresponding to the eastern part of the modern Czech Republic

negle·gō –gere –xī –ctum to neglect

nōn numquam *adv* sometimes

offici·um –ī *n* duty, function

Pannoni·a –ae *f* Pannonia, Roman province, an area roughly corresponding to modern Hungary

parēns parentis *m* parent

patiēns *gen* **patientis** patient, tolerant

perrārō *adv* very rarely

rārō *adv* rarely

rēs reī *f* thing, matter, event

saepe *adv* often

satis *adv* enough

schol·a –ae *f* school

Thessalonīc·a –ae *f* capital of the province of Macedonia in northern Greece

ūtuntur *dep w abl* they use

viti·um –ī *n* vice, bad habit

Section XII
Societās

Adapted from Acts 2:37 & 42

Dīxērunt Petrō et aliīs apostulīs, "Virī et frātrēs, quid faciēmus?" Petrus dīxit, "Perstāte in disciplīnā apostulōrum et societāte."

Adapted from Galatians 2:9

Apostulus Paulus dīxit, "Virī quī erant columnae vīdērunt grātiam quae data est mihi. Ergō dextrās societātis mihi et Barnabas dedērunt."

Adapted from Colossians 4:79

Tychicus cārus frāter et fidēlis minister et cōnservus in Dominō vōbīs omnia dē mē dīcet. Etiam corda vestra cōnsōlābitur. Eum mīsī ad vōs ad haec. Mīsī etiam cum eō Onesimum, cārum et fidēlem frātrem quī est ūnus ex vōbīs.

Onesimus

Adapted from Book of Philemon[*]

Paulus captīvus Iēsū Christī, et Timotheus frāter, Philemonī dīlēctō ministrō nōbīscum, et Appiae sorōrī cārae, et Archippō sociō nostrō, et ecclēsiae, quae in domō tuā est. Grātia vōbīs, et pāx ā Deō Patre nostrō, et Dominō Iēsū Christō. Grātiās agō Deō meō, audiēns cāritātem tuam, et fidem, quam habēs in Dominō Iēsū. Gaudium magnum habuī et cōnsōlātiōnem in cāritāte tuā, frāter.

Ergō quamquam per fidem in Iēsū Christō iubērem tē, propter cāritātem tē beneficium rogō. Paulus senex, captīvus Iēsū Christī, rogō beneficium tē prō meō fīliō in meīs vinculīs Onesimō.

Ōlim Onesimus tibi inūtilis fuit; nunc et mihi et tibi ūtilis erit. Eum tibi remīsī; ergō illum, cor meum, recipe. Voluī eum remanēre mēcum, minister in vinculīs Evangeliī; sed sine cōnsiliō tuō nihil faciam. Factum bonum tuum esse dēbet voluntārium, nōn necessitāte. Fortasse ā tē ad tempus discessit, et nunc aeternum illum recipiēs; nunc nōn est servus, sed cārus frāter, mihi praecipuē, sed magis tibi in carne et in Dominō.

Sī ergō habēs mē socium, recipe eum sīcut mē: sī tibi nocuit aut aliquid dēbet, hoc mihi imputā. Ego Paulus meā manū scrīpsī. Nōn dīcam tibi quod tū tē ipsum, mihi dēbēs. Frāter, ego Christiānus hoc tē rogō: dā mihi gaudium in Dominō.

Scrībō tibi cōnfīdēns: faciēs quod dīcō et magis. Parā hospitium mihi, quia mox propter precēs vestrās fortasse tibi veniam.

---

[*] *This book, like most of the writings of St. Paul, is a letter. Therefore it begins, as letters of the Romans always began, with a greeting or salutation, from sender to receiver: "Paul and Timothy (send greetings) to Philemon, etc."*

Titus Pomponius Atticus (c. 112 BC–c. 32 BC)

Titus Pomponius, who as a man earned the nickname Atticus, was an amazing person and the very embodiment of *societas*, companionship or fellowship, in its highest form. He always seemed to empathize with those in want or peril, and he was always ready to give help, personal or financial. He was the closest friend of Marcus Tullius Cicero, who was a statesman, outstanding speaker, and writer. Cicero wrote a work on friendship called the *Dē Amicītiā* and dedicated it to Atticus. Many of their letters to each other were collected and preserved by Cicero's freedman and personal secretary Tiro.

Titus' father was a wealthy equestrian who was greatly interested in literature and who wanted a fine education for his son. As a boy, Titus and his friend Marcus Tullius Cicero shared a natural capacity for learning. He also had a very agreeable manner and tone, springing from a kindly nature that made him a friend to anyone in trouble. Titus' father died when he was quite young, and the wealthy young man found himself in a very turbulent Roman Republic. Two major political parties had begun to form in Rome, each claiming to espouse the interest of a section of the populace. The *Populares*, or people's party, worked for the plebeians, or commoners; the *Optimates*, or "Best," tried to benefit the patricians or aristocrats. Atticus' own class, the equestrians, stood between the other two. Equestrians were not of aristocratic birth, but they were usually wealthy and influential, so they tended largely to side with the patricians.

Titus was related by marriage to a plebeian tribune named Publius Sulpicius who was assassinated by the patricians, and Titus could easily have been killed also. He had very little interest in the power struggles which seemed to him to offer little but slaughter and misery to both sides, so Titus decided to move a great part of his financial assets to Athens, the major city of the Greek peninsula of Attica, where he made himself very useful to, and consequently very beloved by, the Athenians. He loaned money to the government itself, but wisely and justly, neither charging it outrageous interest nor allowing it to lag behind in repaying the loans. Because of his close ties with Athens and the region surrounding it, he was nicknamed "Atticus."

He helped as many displaced Romans as came to him for help. He was revered and consulted by both sides in the long civil war that convulsed Rome, both while he lived in Athens and after he returned to Rome. Whoever was in power in Rome often slaughtered his enemies, but, even though Atticus had helped those enemies when they were in trouble, he had also helped the victors when they were in trouble. Therefore he was always honored and spared. A list of legendary Roman figures, including Julius Caesar, Mark Antony, and Augustus Caesar, not only honored Atticus, but went to him for advice and counsel.

Adapted from Cornēlius Nepos, *Dē Latīnīs Historicīs* and Marcus Tullius
Cicerō, *Epistulae ad Atticum*

Atticus, ex familiā Rōmānā equestrī nātus, erat puer laetus.
Nōn sōlum pater eius divītiās habuit et disciplīnam amāvit,
sed etiam Atticus erat intellegēns et discendī studiōsus. Dīxit
et scrīpsīt cum ēloquentiā; cor benignum quod eum amīcum
multīs fēcit habuit. Substantiam dīligenter tractāvit, sed
semper dōna pecūniae ieiūnīs aut eīs in perīculō dedit.

Puer Atticus Marcō Tulliō Cicerōnī amīcus erat, et semper
amīcī erant. Cicerō factus est cōnsul Rōmānus et dux Rōmae,
et saepe in perīculō erat; Atticus eī auxilium semper dēdit.

Quandō Atticus iuvenis erat, pater mortuus est. Bellum erat
Rōmae inter Populārēs et Optimātēs, et Atticus nōluit cum
Rōmānīs pugnāre. Athēnīs Atticus habitāvit. Ibi pauperibus et
urbī auxilium dedit, sed prūdēns in auxiliō semper erat.

Nōn sōlum Cicerō, sed etiam Iūlius Caesar, Marcus Brūtus,
Marcus Antōnius, et Augustus Caesar auxilium et cōnsilium
Atticī petīvērunt. Hī virī inimīcī erant, sed nēmō inimīcus
Atticī erat, quod Atticus auxilium benignum omnibus dedit.

Vocabulary for Section XII

aeternum *adv* forever

Athēnīs in Athens, chief city of Attica

benefic·ium –ī *n* kindness, favor

benign·us –a –um kind

carō carnis *f* flesh

column·a –ae *f* column, pillar

cōnfīdēns *gen* cōnfīdentis confident

cōnserv·us –ī *m* fellow servant

cōnsili·um –ī *n* advice

cōnsōlābitur *dep* he will console

cōnsōlāt·iō –ōnis *f* consolation

cor cordis *n* heart

dēbeō dēbēre dēbuī dēbitum to owe

dext·er –ra –rum right; *f* right hand

discēd·ō –ere discessī discessum to depart, to go away

ēloquenti·a –ae *f* eloquence

equest·er –ris –re equestrian, middle class

fortasse *adv* perhaps

gaud·ium –ī *n* joy

grāti·a –ae *f* grace, thanks

hospiti·um –ī *n* welcome, guest room

imperārem *w dat* I might command

imput·ō 1 to charge

inimīc·us –ī *m* enemy

intellegēns *gen* intellegentis intelligent

inūtil·is –e useless

ipsum *pron* yourself

iubērem I might command

magis *adv* more

man·us –ūs *f* hand

mēcum with me

necessit·ās –ātis *f* necessity

nihil *indecl* nothing

nōbīscum with us

ōlim *adv* once

Optimātēs political party of the Roman aristocrats

pāx pācis *f* peace

perst·ō –āre –– to stand firm

Populārēs political party of the Roman common people

prex precis *f* prayer

reman·eō –ēre remānsī –sum to stay, to remain

saepe *adv* often

sine *w abl* without

societ·ās –ātis *f* fellowship, alliance

soci·us –ī *m* partner, companion

sor·or –ōris *f* sister

st·ō –āre stetī statum to stand

studiōs·us –a –um enthusiastic, interested; studiōsus discendī interested in learning

ūtil·is –e useful

vincul·um –ī *n* chain

voluntāri·us –a –um voluntary

Section XIII
Deus et Vir

Adapted from Jeremiah 18:8

Sī illa gēns in quam malum praedīxī paenitentiam dēmōnstrat, ego paenitentiam dē malō quod praedīxī in eam dēmōnstrābō.

Jonah

Adapted from Book of Jonah

Verbum Dominī ad Iōnam vēnit: "Vāde in Ninevēn cīvitātem magnam et praedīc in eam quia malum cōram mē fēcit." Iōnas ā Dominō fūgit, et invēnit nāvem quae ad Tharsis nāvigābat. Ergō Dominus mīsit ventum magnum et facta est tempestās magna in marī. Nāvis in perīculō erat, et virī deōs suōs vocāvērunt. Iōnas dormiēbat, et gubernātor nāvis eī dīxit, "Venī et vocā Deum tuum; fortasse nōs servābit."

Virī sortiēbant, et sors super Iōnam cecidit. "Vidēte," dīxērunt, "Causa malī est. Quis est? Dē quā terrā est?" Iōnas dīxit, "Hebraeus sum, et Dominum Deum quī caelum et terram fēcit timeō."

Virī timuērunt, et dīxērunt, "Quid fēcistī? Effūgistīne Deum tuum? Quid faciēmus?" Iōnas dīxit, "Ēice mē in mare, et mare quiētum erit."

Postquam Iōnas in marī erat, mare quiētum erat. Virī in nāve Dominum timuērunt, et dōna eī dedērunt.

Deus magnum piscem quī Iōnam vorāvit mīsit, et Iōnas in ventre piscis trēs diēs erat. Iōnas ad Dominum Deum suum dē ventre piscis clāmāvit: "Quandō in ventre Īnfernōrum Tibi clāmāvī, mē audīvistī. Aquae Tuae super mē erant. Dīxī, 'Ēiectus sum ā Tē, sed iterum templum sānctum tuum spectābō. Ad extrēma montium dēscendī, et servāvistī vītam meam, Domine Deus. Tē laudābō.' " Dominus imperāvit piscī et piscis ēiēcit Iōnam in terram.

Verbum Dominī ad Iōnam iterum vēnit. "Vāde in Ninevēn cīvitātem magnam et prōnūntiā ibi quae Ego tibi dīxī." Iōnas in Ninevēn vāsit et clāmāvit, "Post quadrāgintā diēs Deus Ninevēn dēlēbit." Virī cīvitātis crēdidērunt Deō: prōnūntiāvērunt iēiūnium et omnēs vestēs ciliciī habuērunt. Rēx Ninevēs solium relīquit et, in cinere sedēns, vestēs ciliciī habuit. Rēx prōnūntiāvit, "Nec homō nec animal edent; omnēs in ciciliciō tegentur, et omnēs Deō clāmābunt. Omnēs ā malō āversābuntur." Deus vīdit operās eōrum. Vīdit eōs ā malō āversārī, et mala eīs Deus nōn fēcit.

Iōnas īrācundus erat. Dīxit, "Nōnne dīxī in patriā meā, 'Deus misericordiam magnam habet; benignus est; nōn vult facere mala.' Ergō fūgī ad mare. Nunc, Domine, cape vītam meam. Mihi mors melior est quam vīta." Deus dīxit, "Prōdestne tibi esse īrācundus?" "Prōdest," dīxit Iōnas.

Iōnas ē cīvitāte vāsit et umbrāculum sibi fēcit. Sēdit in umbrāculō et spectāvit cīvitātem. Deus fēcit vīneam quae ascendit super caput Iōnae. In umbrā vīneae Iōnas laetus erat.

Deus vermem mīsit, et vermis vīneae nocuit. Vīnea mortua est, et sōl caput Iōnae torrēbat. Iōnas dīxit, "Mihi mors melior est quam vīta." Deus dīxit, "Prōdestne tibi esse īrācundus?" "Prōdest," dīxit Iōnas.

Deus dīxit, "Tū dolēs dē vīneā in quā nōn labōrāvistī; neque fēcistī. Crēvit in ūnā nocte et ūnā nocte mortua est. Nōnne servābō Ninevēn in quā sunt multī hominēs et multa animālia?"

Vocabulary for Section XIII

āversābuntur they will turn away from; āversārī to turn away

caus·a –ae f cause, reason

cilic·ium –ī n sackcloth, clothing worn for penance

cin·is –eris m ashes

clām·ō 1 to shout, to cry out

dēl·eō –ēre –ēvī –ētum to destroy

dol·eō –ēre –uī dolitum to grieve

dorm·iō –īre –īvī –ītum to sleep

effug·iō –ere effūgī –– to flee

extrēma –ōrum n pl last part, deepest part

gubernāt·or –ōris m pilot

iēiūn·ium –ī n fast

imper·ō 1 to command

Īnfern·a –ōrum n pl the Underworld

Iōn·as –ae m Jonah

mar·e –is n sea

melior melius better

nāvis nāvis f ship

nāvig·ō 1 to sail

Ninev·ē –ēs f Nineveh, the ancient capital of Assyria acc Ninevēn

nox noctis f night

paenitenti·a –ae f repentance

praedīc·ō –ere praedīxī praedictum to predict, to command beforehand

prō·sum –desse –fuī –– w dat to be good for

quadrāgintā indecl forty

quiēt·us –a –um quiet, tranquil

sed·eō –ēre –ī sessum to sit; sedēns sitting

sibi for oneself

sōl sōlis m sun

sol·ium –ī n throne, chair

sors sortis f lot, decision by lots; sortīre to cast lots

teg·ō –ere tēxī tēctum to cover; tegentur they will be covered

tempest·ās –ātis f storm

templ·um –ī n temple

Tharsis indecl Tarshish, an ancient city or trading destination

torr·eō –ēre –uī tōstum to scorch, to burn

umbrācul·um –ī n shade, shelter

vent· er –ris m stomach, belly

vent·us –ī m wind

verm·is –is m worm

vor·ō 1 to swallow, to devour

Section XIV
Vir Fideī

Adapted from Proverbs 28:20

Vir fidēlis beātitūdinēs magnās habēbit.

Adapted from 1 Corinthians 16:3

Spectāte, stāte in fidē, vīvite virī, este fortēs.

Adapted from Daniel 1, 5, and 6

Nabuchodonosor rēx Babylōnis Ierosolymam cēpit. Multa
ē domō Deī et multōs Hebraeōs in terram Sennaar portāvit.
Rēx dīxit ministrō, "Cupiō Hebraeōs iuvenēs ē sanguine rēgis
et ducum, puerōs in quibus nōn vitia sunt, in domō meā.
Ēducā eōs cum disciplīnā bonā. Discent litterās et linguam
Chaldaeōrum, et stābunt cōram rēge. Dā eīs cibum et vīnum
dē mēnsā rēgis, et fortēs et intellegentēs erunt. Post trēs annōs
cōram rēge stābunt."

Inter Hebraeōs puerōs erant Daniēl, Ananias, Misahēl,
et Azarias. Daniēl nōluit edere cibum et bibere vīnum dē
mēnsā rēgis. Quandō Daniēl hoc ministrō dīxit, minister
dīxit, "Timeō rēgem meum dominum; sī nōn fortēs estis sīcut
aliī puerī, erit īrācundus." Daniēl dīxit, "Temptā nōs decem
diēs. Edēmus legūmina et bibēmus aquam. Deinde vidē num
tam fortēs sīmus quam aliī puerī." Post decem diēs Daniēl,
Ananias, Misahēl, et Azarias meliōrem vultum quam aliī puerī
habuērunt. Minister dedit omnibus puerīs legūmina et aquam.
Daniēlī et amīcīs eius dedit Deus scientiam et sapientiam.
Daniēlī etiam intellegentiam omnium vīsiōnum et somniōrum
dedit.

Baltassar rēx, fīlius Nabuchodonosoris, bibit vīnum ē vāsīs
aurī et argentī quae Nabuchodonosor pater eius dē templō
Deī in Ierosolymā portāverat. In mūrō manus appāruit et
scrīpsit verba arcāna. Nēmō scīvit verba arcāna, et rēgīna
rēgī dīxit, "Rēx, in aeternum vīve. Est vir in rēgnō tuō quī
spīritum deōrum sānctōrum habet in eō. In diēbus tuī patris
Nabuchodonosoris scientia et sapientia inventae sunt in eō."

Rēx Daniēlī dīxit, "Esne Daniēl ē captīvīs Hebraeīs quōs
pater meus portāvit hūc? Sī verba arcāna mihi explicābis,
dabō tibi aurum et argentum." Daniēl dīxit, "Dā aliīs aurum et
argentum tuum. Verba dīcunt, 'Deus rēgnum tuum termināvit;
tū inventus est inops. Rēgnum tuum datum est Mēdīs et
Persīs.'" Illā nocte mortuus est Baltassar rēx et Dārīus Mēdus
recēpit rēgnum.

Rēx Dārīus regnō satrapās centum vīgintī praefēcit, et eīs
prīncipēs trēs praefēcit ē quibus Daniēl prīmus erat. Prīncipēs
et satrapae dēlēre Daniēlem cupīvērunt, et petīvērunt vitia
in eō. Nihil invēnērunt; Daniēl fidēlis rēgī erat. Ergō virī illī
dīxērunt, "Nōn inveniēmus Daniēle hōc vitium nisi fortasse in
officiō Deī eius."

Vēnērunt ad rēgem et dīxērunt, "Rēx, in aeternum vīve.
Omnēs prīncipēs et satrapae regnī tuī cupīvērunt ēdictum
in honōre tuō." Ēdictum dicet, "Quisquis petit beneficium
magnum ā deō aut homine nisi ā tē, rēx, īnsequentēs trīgintā
diēs vādet in latibulum leōnum." Rēx scrīpsit ēdictum in lēge
Mēdīs et Persīs quae numquam potest mūtārī.

Daniēl ēdictum vīdit, sed tamen in domō suā Deum
Dominum precibus ōrāvit. Prīncipēs et satrapae rēgī dīxērunt,
"Nōnne ēdictum dīcit 'Quisquis petit beneficium magnum ā
deō aut homine nisi ā tē, rēx, īnsequentēs trīgintā diēs vādet in
latibulum leōnum?'"

Rēx dīxit, "Vērum est, et est in lēge Mēdīs et Persīs quae
numquam potest mūtārī." Virī dīxērunt, "Daniēl Hebraeus
nōn cūrāvit dē lēge tuā et dē ēdictō tuō. Cōtīdiē Deum suum
precibus ōrāvit."

Rēx dolēbat, sed propter lēgem posuit Daniēlem in latibulō
leōnum. Dīxit, "Deus tuus servābit tē." Illā nocte rēx nōn
ēdit, et nōn dormīvit. Māne rēx ad latibulum leōnum vāsit et
vocāvit, "Servāvitne tē Deus tuus, Daniēl?" Daniēl dīxit, "Rēx,
in aeternum vīve."

Rēx laetus erat. Posuit illōs virōs quī accūsāvērunt
Daniēlem in latibulō leōnum et prōnūntiāvit, "Rēgnum meum
Deum Daniēlis timēbit, quod est Deus vīvēns."

Vocabulary for Section XIV

accūs·ō 1 to accuse

ann·us –ī *m* year

appār·eō –ēre –uī –itum to appear

arcān·us –a –um mysterious, secret

argent·um –ī *n* silver

aur·um –ī *n* gold

Babylōn Babylōnis *f* the city of Babylon

Baltassar Baltassaris *m* Belshazzar, king of Babylon

beātitūd·ō –inis *f* blessing

bib·ō –ere bibī bibitum to drink

cap·iō –ere cēpī captum to take, to capture

centum vīgintī *indecl* one hundred and twenty

Chaldae·ī –ōrum *m pl* Chaldeans, a people of Assyria learned in astronomy

Daniēl Daniēlis *m* Daniel

decem *indecl* ten

dēl·eō –ēre –ēvī –ētum to destroy

ēdict·um –ī *n* proclamation, edict

explic·ō 1 to explain

hūc *adv* to this place

inop·s –is wanting, lacking

īnsequ·ēns –entis next, following

intellegenti·a –ae *f* understanding

latibul·um –ī *n* den

legūm·en –inis *n* vegetable

litter·a –ae *f* letter of the alphabet; *pl* letters, literature

Mēd·ī –ōrum *m pl* Medes, ancient people of the Middle East

mūr·us –ī *m* wall

Nabuchodonosor Nabuchodonosoris *m* Nebuchadnezzar, king of Babylon

num *conj* whether

ōr·ō 1 to entreat

Pers·ae –ārum *m pl* Persians

potest mūtārī can be changed; *lit* is able to be changed

prīnc·eps –cipis *m* chief, leader

propter *w acc* on account of, because of, according to

rēgīn·a –ae *f* queen

sapienti·a –ae *f* wisdom

satrap·a –ae *m* governor, viceroy

scienti·a –ae *f* knowledge

sīmus we may be

somn·ium –ī *n* dream

tam ... quam as ... as

termin·ō 1 to mark the boundaries of

trīgintā *indecl* thirty

vās·um –ī *n* vessel, utensil

vīn·um, –ī *n* wine

vīsi·ō –ōnis *f* apparition, vision

vult·us –ūs *m* appearance, face

LIST OF ABBREVIATIONS

abl	ablative	*indecl*	indeclinable
abl obj	ablative object	*infin*	infinitive
acc	accusative	*lit*	literally
adj	adjective	*loc*	locative
adv	adverb	*m*	masculine
conj	conjunction	*m pl*	masculine plural
dat	dative	*n*	neuter
dat obj	dative object	*n pl*	neuter plural
def	defective verb	*pl*	plural
dep	deponent verb	*prep*	preposition
f	feminine	*pron*	pronoun
f pl	feminine plural	*semi-dep*	semideponent
gen	genitive	*v imper*	impersonal verb
id	idiom, a word or phrase with a special meaning	*voc*	vocative; used when speaking to someone
imp	imperative, command		

APPENDIX I

Pronunciation Guide
(American Scholastic)

Latin words generally have no silent letters; exceptions are loan words from other languages, such as those with an internal silent *h*. The words break up into syllables and can be pronounced one syllable at a time. There are as many syllables as there are vowels or diphthongs. The next to last syllable is stressed if it has a long vowel or is followed by two consonants. If neither of these things is true, the third from the last syllable is accented.

Here is a simple guide to the sounds. The long vowels are usually twice as long as the short; they sound like the vowels in these English words:

Long

ā as in father	sānc' tus
ē as in they	rēx
ī as in machine	nī' dus
ō as in vote	nōn
ū as in rule	iūs' tus

Short

a as the first sound in aha	par tī' re
e as in bet	an' gel us
i as in bit	vi dē' re
o as in bottle	vo' cat
u as in but	hi run' di nis

Diphthongs (two vowels pronounced very quickly together)

ae –ah –ā	as in aisle	quae
au –ah –oo	as in out	tau' rus
oe –oh –ā	as in spoil	poe' na

Consonants

Most are the same as English. Here are the notable exceptions.

c is always hard as in cake	fa' ci ō
g is always hard as in get	cō gi tā' re
s is always hissed; never *z*	a' si na
v is pronounced *w*	vī' pe rae

APPENDIX II
Latin Word Endings in the Earliest Stories
(for Sections I, II, and III)

In English the placement of words in a thought or sentence is shown by the order in which the words come. Subject is the name given to words that fill the slot occupied by "the wolf" in the sentence "the wolf sees the lamb." Direct object is the name given to words that fill the slot occupied by "the lamb" in the sentence "the wolf sees the lamb."

Verbs also can be identified by the slot they fill in a sentence. We know that "see" is a verb because it tells what the subject noun does to the direct object noun. Which of the following words can go in the verb slot?

sheep, chases, large, ignores, slowly, orange

We cannot make a sensible statement by saying "the wolf large the lamb" or "the wolf slowly the lamb." Only the second and fourth word in the list can make a sentence when placed in the slot. Therefore the second and fourth words are verbs.

In English the subject and words that go with it usually come first, the verb comes second, and the direct object and words that go with it come last. In Latin the place of words in a thought unit or sentence (when translated into English) is shown by how the words are spelled.

Look at the forms of "asina"—"donkey":

Asina prophētam portat. The donkey carries the prophet.

Angelus asinam vīdet. The angel sees the donkey.

The subject of a sentence may end in various letters, but the direct objects in the earliest stories end in "m." A noun following a little word called a preposition may end with any vowel—"ā," "ō," " ī," "ē," "e," or "ū" in the earliest stories. For example "in sānctō monte"—"on the holy mountain" is a phrase in the Latin ablative case telling where something is located. The Latin noun of address generally changes from "us" to "e" on nouns that refer to the masculine.

When the Lord is spoken to, the word "Dominus" becomes "Domine." "Deus"—"God"—as an address, however, remains "Deus." The syllable "–ne" on the end of the first word means that the sentence is a question; "–ne" itself has no translation. The syllable is added because Latin did not use punctuation marks such as question marks.

Adjectives (words which tell about the nouns) in the early sections end in "s" or "m" if the word which they tell about is marked *m* or *n* in the glossary, and with "a" or "m" if the word is marked *f* in the glossary. They generally have the same ending as the word they tell about.

Notice that the verb also changes. Look at the verb charts given below carefully. It is obvious that the verb ending "ō" or "m" means "I." "Portō" means "I carry," "portās" means "you carry," and so on. "Sum" means "I am."

The words "he," "she," or "it" are not used when a subject such as "angelus" or "asina" is present.

Irregular Verb
esse "to be"

sum – I am	sumus – we are
es – you are	estis – you (plural) are
est – he, she, it is	sunt – they are

Present Tense of Verb
portāre "to carry"

portō – I carry	portāmus – we carry
portās – you carry	portātis – you (plural) carry
portat – he, she, it carries	portant – they carry

APPENDIX III
Noun Endings

The endings of nouns, like those of verbs, show the place a word holds in the sentence (when translated into English) or thought unit and the relationship between the noun and other words in the sentence. This relationship between the spelling of a word and its placement in a thought unit is best demonstrated in English by pronouns, words which stand in the place of a noun.

	English	Latin
Nominative (Subject) pronoun	he	is
Possessive pronoun	his	eius
Objective pronoun	him	eum

In Latin, the objective pronouns are divided into indirect object, direct object, and object of preposition; thus there are two more forms: "eī" which means "to" or "for him" and "eō" which means "by" or "with him."

The structure of a Latin noun such as "agnus" looks like this:

Nominative	agnus	the lamb (does something)
Genitive (possessive)	agnī	of the lamb
Dative (indirect object)	agnō	to, for the lamb
Accusative (direct object)	agnum	(something does) the lamb
Ablative (object of prep)	agnō	by, with, from the lamb

The ablative case is very often used with a preposition, a little word that shows the relationship between the word which follows it and something else in the sentence or thought.

Sample:
prō agnō – for or on behalf of the lamb

"Agnus" demonstrates only one of several sets of nouns, so the ablative case may end with any vowel—"ā," "e," "ē," "ī," "ō," or "ū." Examples are "dē agnō"—about the lamb; "in viā"—in the road. The preposition may be followed by a noun in the accusative case. An example is "ad Antiochiam"—to Antioch.

The nouns discussed above are all singular. Nouns also have plural forms, so that the entire structure of "agnus" looks like this:

Second Declension Masculine

		Singular		Plural
Nominative	agnus	the lamb (does something)	agnī	the lambs (do something)
Genitive	agnī	of the lamb	agnōrum	of the lambs
Dative	agnō	to, for the lamb	agnīs	to, for the lambs
Accusative	agnum	(something does) the lamb	agnōs	(something does) the lambs
Ablative	agnō	by, with, from the lamb	agnīs	by, with from the lambs

First Declension Feminine

		Singular		Plural
Nominative	via	the road (does something)	viae	the roads (do something)
Genitive	viae	of the road	viārum	of the roads
Dative	viae	to, for the road	viīs	to, for the roads
Accusative	viam	(something does) the road	viās	(something does) the roads
Ablative	viā	by, with, from the road	viīs	by, with, from the roads

The second declension pattern has been given here first because the *Artes Latinae* learning format concentrates for a long time on subject nouns with the letter "s" for an ending. There are numerous variations on the patterns above. For the earliest lessons, we will watch for position of words. The subjects will often come first, other phrases such as genitive and dative second, the direct objects next, and verbs often last. Exceptions to this are questions, which generally begin with the verb, and sentences using forms of the linking verb "sum," which may come at various places in the sentence. Prepositional phrases, which are introduced by a preposition, may occur at any point in the sentence.

Sample sentences:

Pater dat puerō agnum.	Father gives a lamb to the boy.
Dat agnō cibum.	He gives food to the lamb.
Dat agnō puerī cibum.	He gives food to the lamb of the boy.
Pater dat in viā agnō puerī cibum.	Father gives food to the lamb of the boy in the road.

APPENDIX IV
Variation in Noun Endings
(for Section IV and Subsequent Sections)

We are now ready to experience more variation with noun endings. Latin has five different declensions of nouns, but we shall concentrate for the present on the forms that remain fairly regular throughout the five declensions.

The accusative case, which gives us direct objects and some objects of prepositions, ends with "m" if the noun is singular or "s" if the noun is plural unless it is of the neuter gender. Here is a neuter noun structure that is closely related to the first pattern we met, the second declension masculine:

		Second Declension Neuter		
		Singular		**Plural**
Nominative	verbum	the word (does something)	verba	the words (do something)
Genitive	verbī	of the word	verbōrum	of the words
Dative	verbō	to, for the word	verbīs	to, for the words
Accusative	verbum	(something does) the word	verba	(something does) the words
Ablative	verbō	by, with the word	verbīs	by, with the words

Notice that the neuter nominative and accusative forms are the same, and that both their plurals end in "a." This will be true of all neuter nouns, regardless of the declension into which they fall. Remember from Appendix I that the ablative singular may end in "ā," "ō," "ī," "e," "ē," or "ū." Looking back over the three noun declension patterns given thus far, notice that the dative and ablative plurals end with "īs." The context of the sentence shows whether this ending is dative—"to" or "for"—or ablative, which can mean "by" or "with" or can be the object of a preposition. The genitive case singular, which means "of," is always the second form given in the glossary. Notice that genitive plurals end in "ōrum" or "ārum."

Sample sentences:

Verba puerōrum bona sunt.   The words of the boys are good.

Dīcit puerīs verba bona.   He says good words to the boys.

Special Note:

Some verbs take a direct object in the dative, or occasionally the ablative, case. Such verbs will be marked *dat obj (dative object)* or *abl obj (ablative object).*

APPENDIX V

Further Variations in Noun Endings

We have seen the declension patterns for nouns of the first and second declensions. The third, fourth, and fifth declensions have various endings in the nominative singular and long "ēs" or "a" in the nominative plural. Their dative singulars will generally end with "ī"; their ablative singulars, as seen above, may end with any vowel. Dative and ablative plurals end with "īs" for the first two declensions and with "bus" for the other three. One example is below:

Third Declension Masculine and Feminine

	Singular			Plural	
Nominative	vēritās	the truth (does something)	vēritātēs	the truths (do something)
Genitive	vēritātis	of the truth	vēritātum	of the truths
Dative	vēritātī	to, for the truth	vēritātibus	to, for the truths
Accusative	vēritātem	(something does) the truth	vēritātēs	(something does) the truths
Ablative	vēritāte	by, with the truth	vēritātibus	by, with the truths

Sample sentences:

Dat cāritātem.	He gives love.
Dat cāritāte.	He gives with love.
Dat cāritātis.	He gives of his love.

Appendix VI
Forms of Adjectives

Adjectives must agree with the nouns they modify in number, gender, and case. This means, for example, that they must be plural if their noun is plural, feminine if their noun is feminine, and accusative if their noun is accusative. Many adjectives follow the pattern of "agnus," "via," and "verbum," in which case the forms given in the glossary will be, for example, "magnus," "magna," and "magnum." Other adjectives follow the general pattern of "vēritās." Such adjectives will generally have forms such as "fortis," "forte." For such adjectives "fortis" goes with masculine and feminine nouns and "forte" goes with neuter ones. Some adjectives such as "prūdēns" will have only one nominative form; they will be listed in the glossary as follows: "prūdēns *gen* prūdentis." Some adjectives will end with "er" in the nominative masculine singular. We must then look to the second, or feminine nominative, form to see which pattern they follow. An example is "pulcher," "pulchra," "pulchrum."

Sample sentences:

Videō asinam pulchram.	I see a pretty donkey.
Puer fortis asinam fidelem cūrat.	The brave boy cares for the faithful donkey.

APPENDIX VII

Principal Parts of Verbs; Perfect Tense Active; Participles

In Appendix II we have seen verbs in the present tense; that is, they tell what is happening in present time. These are made from the first and second principal parts of the verb, with personal endings added to indicate who is doing the action.

For the perfect, or simple past tense, the third principal part and another set of personal endings are used.

The fourth principal part is a participle (a verb part which can act as a modifier or adjective). It is also used in the Perfect Tense Passive (see Appendix IX).

Sample sentence:
Īnsulam dēsertam invēnimus.   We found a deserted island.

The present participle, made by dropping the "–re" from the second principal part and adding "–ns –ntis," is translated with the English participle ending in "–ing."

Sample sentence:
Parentēs amantēs īnfantem cūrant.   The loving parents care for the baby.

portō I carry **portāre** to carry **portāvī** I carried **portātum** having been carried

Present Tense of Verb

portō – I carry	portāmus – we carry
portās – you carry	portātis – you (plural) carry
portat – he, she, it carries	portant – they carry

Perfect Tense of Verb

portāvī – I carried, have carried	portāvimus – we carried, have carried
portāvistī – you carried, have carried	portāvistis – you (plural) carried, have carried
portāvit – he, she it, carried, has carried	portāvērunt – they carried, have carried

Present Tense of sum, esse fuī, futūrus: to be

sum – I am	sumus – we are
es – you are	estis – you are
est – he, she, it is	sunt – they are

Perfect (Complete Past) Tense of sum

fuī – I was, have been	fuimus – we were, have been
fuistī – you were, have been	fuistis – you (plural) were, have been
fuit – he, she, it was, has been	fuērunt – they were, have been

Imperfect (Incomplete Past) Tense of sum

eram – I was, used to be	erāmus – we were, used to be
erās – you were, used to be	erātis – you (plural) were, used to be
erat – he, she, it was, used to be	erant – they were, used to be

APPENDIX VIII
Future Tense

When a sentence needs to tell something that will happen in the future, Latin has two ways of making special verbs for that. Latin verbs are divided into groups called conjugations according to the vowel (capitalized below) found on the second principal part just before the letters "re."

Samples:

1st Conjugation

1st Principal Part	2nd PP	3rd PP	4th PP
portō I carry	portĀre to carry	portāvī I carried	portātum having been carried

2nd Conjugation

dēbeō I owe	dēbĒre to owe	dēbuī I owed	dēbitum having been owed

3rd Conjugation

regō I rule	regEre to rule	rēxī I ruled	rēctum having been ruled

4th Conjugation

inveniō I find	invenĪre to find	invēnī I found	inventum having been found

Verbs of the 1st and 2nd conjugation take the second principal part, drop the "re" and add these personal endings:

- –bō I shall
- –bis you will
- –bit he will
- –bimus we shall
- –bitis you (plural) will
- –bunt they will

portābō – I shall carry
portābis – you will carry
portābit – he, she, it will carry

portābimus – we shall carry
portābitis – you (plural) will carry
portābunt – they will carry

Verbs of the 3rd and 4th conjugations drop the "re" and add these endings:

–am I shall	**ēmus** we will
–ēs you will	**ētis** you (plural) will
–et he will	**ent** they will

regam I shall rule	**regēmus we shall rule**
regēs you will rule	**regētis you (plural) will rule**
reget he will rule	**regent they will rule**

Notice that "dēbēs" and "regēs" look alike, but they are in different conjugations.

The 2nd principal part of "dēbeō" is "debĒre," and so "dēbēs" means "you owe."

The second principal part of "regō" is "rēgEre," and so "regēs" means "you will rule."

Appendix IX
Perfect Tense Passive

Sometimes we want to tell not what the subject did, but what was done to the subject. In the sentence "the wolf was seen by the lamb" the wolf has the same place in the sentence that he had in "the wolf saw the lamb," but he is no longer doing what is done. Now he is still the subject, but he is no longer the actor. These forms are made in Latin with the perfect passive participle, which is the fourth principal part of the verb, and the present tense of sum.

Sample sentences
1. The wolf saw the lamb. Lupus agnum vīdit.
2. The wolf was seen by the lamb. Lupus ab agnō vīsus est.

Perfect Tense Passive

relictus sum	I was left	relictī sumus	we were left
relictus es	you were left	relictī estis	you (plural) were left
relictus est	he was left	relictī sunt	they were left

LATIN TO ENGLISH GLOSSARY

ā, ab *prep w abl* from

ac *conj* as well as, and also

accēd·ō –ere accessī accessum to approach

accinct·us –a –um girded, belted

accūs·ō 1 to accuse

acer·bus –a –um harsh, bitter; **acerbē** harshly

ad *prep w acc* to

adolēsc·ō –ere adolēvī adultum to grow up

aedific·ō 1 to build

Aegypt ·us –ī *f* Egypt

aequ·us –a –um equal, just; **aequē** justly

aeternum *adv* forever, for all time

a·ger –grī *m* field, farm

agell·um –ī *n* little field, little farm

agn·us –ī *m* lamb

agricultūr·a –ae *f* agriculture, farming

ali·quis –quid someone, anyone, something

ali·us –a –ud other

altar·ia –ium *n pl* altar

amābil·is –e lovable; **amābilia** lovable things

Amalek *indecl* Amalekites, a nomadic tribe

amīc·us –ī *m* friend

am·or –ōris *m* love

angel·us –ī *m* angel

anim·a –ae *f* life, soul

animal animālis *n* animal

annūnti·ō 1 to proclaim, to announce

ann·us –ī *m* year

ante *prep with acc* before

Antiochi·a –ae *f* city of Antioch

an·us –ūs *f* old woman

apostul·us –ī *m* one sent with the Good News, apostle, missionary

appār·eō –ēre –uī –itum to appear

apud *prep w acc* at

arbor arboris *f* tree

arcān·us –a –um mysterious, secret

argent·um –ī *n* silver

Arimathae·a –ae *f* the city of Arimathaea

arm·a –ōrum *n pl* weapons, arms

ascend·ō –ere –ī ascēnsum to ascend

asin·a –ae *f* donkey

aud·iō –īre –īvī –ītum to hear

aur·um –ī *n* gold

aut *conj* or; **aut ... aut** either ... or

auxil·ium –ī *n* help, aid

āversābuntur they will turn away from; **āversārī** to turn away

āvert·ō –ere –tī āversum to turn away

avuncul·us –ī *m* uncle

Babylōn Babylōnis *f* the city of Babylon

Baltassar Baltassaris *m* Belshazzar, king of Babylon

barbar·us –ī *m* barbarian, foreigner

Barnabas *indecl* Barnabas

beātitūd·ō –inis *f* blessing

belliger·us –ī *m* man of war

bell·um –ī *n* war

bene *adv* well

benefic·ium –ī *n* kindness, favor

benign·us –a –um kind

Bethlehemitic·us –a –um pertaining to Bethelehem, of Bethelehem

bib·ō –ere bibī bibitum to drink

bon·us –a –um good; *n pl* **bona** good things

cad·ō –ere cecidī cāsum to fall

cael·um –ī *n* heaven, sky

Caleb *indecl* an Israelite

cap·iō –ere cēpī captum to take, to capture

captīv·us –ī *m* captive, prisoner

cārect·um –ī *n* a bed of reeds

cārit·ās –ātis *f* generous love

carō carnis *f* flesh

cār·us –a –um dear

castīg·ō 1 to reprove, to scold

castit·ās –ātis *f* purity

caus·a –ae *f* cause, reason

cēl·ō 1 to conceal

cēns·or –ōris *m* censor (*one of two officials elected every five years to take census and censor morals*)

centum *indecl* one hundred

centum mīlium *n* hundred thousand

centum vīgintī *indecl* one hundred and twenty

centuri·ō –ōnis *m* Roman commander of one hundred soldiers, centurion

Chaldae·ī –ōrum *m pl* Chaldeans, a people of Assyria learned in astronomy

Chanaān *indecl* Canaan

Christiān·us –ī *m* follower of Christ, a Christian

cib·us –ī *m* food

cilic·ium –ī *n* sackcloth, clothing worn for penance

cin·is –eris *m* ashes

cīvit·ās –ātis *f* city, state

clām·ō 1 to shout, to cry out

claud·us –a –um lame, crippled

coep·ī –isse –tum *def* to begin

cōgit·ō 1 to consider, to think on; **cōgitāte** *imp* think on!

cognōsc·ō –ere cognōvī cognitum to know

column·a –ae *f* column, pillar

committ·ō –ere commīsī commissum to entrust

cōnfīdēns *gen* **cōnfīdentis** confident

cōnserv·us –ī *m* fellow servant

cōnsil·ium –ī *n* advice

cōnsōlābitur *dep* he will console

cōnsōlāti·ō –ōnis *f* consolation

Cōnstantīn·us –ī *m* Constantine, Roman commander and emperor

cōnsul cōnsulis *m* consul (*one of the two highest elected officials in Rome; elected annually*)

cōnsūm·ō –ere cōnsūmpsī cōnsūmptum to use up, to waste

contemn·ō –ere contempsī contemptum to despise

contumēliōs·us –a –um insulting

conversāti·o –ōnis *f* interaction

cor cordis *n* heart

cōram *prep w abl* in the presence of, before

corp·us –oris *n* body

cōtīdiē *adv* daily

crēd·ō –ere crēdidī crēditum to entrust; *w dat* to believe, to believe in

crēsc·ō –ere crēvī crētum to grow, to increase

cui to whom

cum *prep w abl* with

cup·iō –ere cupīvī cupītum to want, to desire

cūr *adv* why

cūr·ō 1 to take care of, to heal

Cyrill·us –ī *m* Cyril, Apostle to the Slavs

Daniēl Daniēlis *m* Daniel

Dāvīd Dāvīdis *m* David

dē *prep w abl* from, about, concerning

dēb·eō –ēre –uī –itum to owe

decem *indecl* ten

Decem·ber –bris *m* December

dēcrēsc·ō –ere dēcrēvī dēcrētum to decrease

dēfess·us –a –um tired, weary

dēflect·ō –ere dēflexī dēflectum to turn aside

deinde *adv* then

dēl·eō –ēre –ēvī –ētum to destroy

dēmōnstr·ō 1 to show, to demonstrate

dēnār·ius –ī *m* small coin, daily wage of a laborer in the first century

dē·pōnō –pōnere –posuī –positum to put down, to lay down

dēscend·ō –ere –ī dēscēnsum to go down, to descend

dēser·ō –ere dēseruī dēsertum to desert, to abandon

dex·ter –tra –trum right; *f* right hand

De·us –ī *m* God

diācon·us –ī *m* minister, servant of the church, deacon

dīc·ō –ere dīxī dictum to say

di·ēs –ēī *m* day

dign·us –a –um worthy, proper; *w abl* worthy (of)

dīlēcti·ō –ōnis *f* love

dīligēns *gen* **dīligentis** industrious, diligent; **dīligenter** diligently

dīlig·ō –ere dīlēxī dīlēctum to love above all others, even oneself

discēd·ō –ere discessī discessum to depart, to go away

disciplīn·a –ae *f* teaching, education

discipul·us –ī *m* learner, pupil, disciple

disc·ō –ere didicī – – to learn **studiōsus discendī** eager to learn

dīvid·ō –ere dīvīsī dīvīsum to divide

dīvīti·ae –ārum *f pl* riches

dō dare dedī datum to give

doc·eō –ēre –uī –tum to teach (*takes two direct objects*); **doct·us –a –um** learned

dol·eō –ēre doluī dolitum to grieve

Domin·us –ī *m* the Lord God

dom·us –ūs *f* home, house

dōn·um –ī *n* gift

dorm·iō –īre –īvī –ītum to sleep

dū·cō –cere –xī –ctum to lead

dum *conj* while

du·o –ae –o two

duodecim *indecl* twelve

dux ducis *m* leader

ē, ex *prep w abl* from, out of

ecclēsi·a –ae *f* church

ēdict·um –ī *n* proclamation, edict

ed·ō –ere ēdī ēsum to eat

ēduc·ō 1 to bring up, to raise

effug·iō –ere effūgī – – to flee

effūs·us –a –um immoderate

ego *pron* I

ē·iciō –icere –iēcī –iectum to throw out, to eject

eius *pron* his, hers, its; **eī** to, for him; **eum** him

element·a –ōrum *n pl* alphabet

ēlig·ō –ere ēlēgī ēlēctum to choose;
   ēlēgite *imp* choose

ēloquēns *gen* **ēloquentis** eloquent, well-
   expressed

ēloquenti·a –ae *f* eloquence

ēmend·ō 1 to correct

eō *pron* him

ephod *indecl* a Jewish vestment

epīscop·us –ī *m* bishop

epistul·a –ae *f* a letter

epul·um –ī *n* banquet

equest·er –ris –re equestrian, middle
   class

ergō *adv* therefore

erit he, she, it will be

erō I shall be

err·ō 1 to make a mistake, to wander

error errōris *m* mistake

esse to be

este *imp* be

et *conj* and; **et . . . et** both . . . and

etiam *adv* also

Evangeli·um –ī *n* Good News, Gospel

exempl·um –ī *n* example

explic·ō 1 to explain

exspect·ō 1 to await, to expect

extrēm·a –ōrum *n pl* last part, deepest
   part

fābul·a –ae *f* story

faci·ō –ere fēcī factum to do, to make;
   fac *imp* do

fam·ā –ae *f* report, reputation

fam·ēs –is *f* hunger, famine

famili·a –ae *f* family, household

fēmin·a –ae *f* woman

ferē *adv* almost

ferō ferre tulī lātum to bear, to endure,
   to carry; **fert** he endures

fiet it shall be done

fidēl·is –e faithful

fid·ēs –ēī *f* faith

fīli·a –ae *f* daughter

fīli·us –ī *m* son; *voc* **fīlī**

firm·ō 1 to strengthen

fiscell·a –ae *f* small basket

flūm·en –inis *n* river

flu·ō –ere –xī –xum to flow

foed·us –eris *n* agreement, pact, treaty;
   foedus īcere to make a pact or treaty

fōrm·a –ae *f* form, shape, likeness, beauty

fortasse *adv* perhaps

fort·is –e brave, strong

fortitūd·ō –inis *f* strength

frā·ter –tris *m* brother

frātern·us –a –um brotherly

frīg·us –oris *n* cold

fruct·us –ūs *m* fruit

fug·iō –ere fūgī fugitum to run away, to
   flee, to flee from

gaud·ium –ī *n* joy, gladness

gemm·a –ae *f* jewel

generāti·ō –ōnis *f* generation

gēns gentis *f* clan, family, tribe, people,
   nation

Graeci·a –ae *f* Greece

Graec·us –a –um Greek

grati·a –ae *f* grace, thanks

grātiās tibi agō I thank you

gubernāt·or –ōris *m* pilot

hab·eō –ēre –uī –itum to have, to hold,
   to use

habit·ō 1 to live, to dwell

haud exceptō id included; *lit* by no
   means left out

Hebrae·us –ī *m* Hebrew

herb·a –ae f grass

hīc adv here

hic haec hoc this; n pl haec these things

hirund·ō –inis f swallow (a bird)

Hispān·us –ī m Spaniard

histori·a –ae f history

hodiē adv today

hom·ō –inis m human being, man; pl people

honest·ās –ātis f integrity

honest·us –a –um honorable, respected

honor honōris m honor

hōr·a –ae f hour

hosp·es –itis m host, guest

hospit·ium –ī n welcome, guest room

hūc adv to this place

huic to this

ibi adv there

ībō I shall go

identidem adv again and again

iēiūn·ium –ī n fast

iēiūn·us –a –um hungry, fasting

Iericho indecl Jericho

Ierosolym·a –ae f the city of Jerusalem

Iēsus Iēsū m gen dat abl voc Iēsu acc Iēsum Jesus

ignis ignis m fire

ill·e –a –ud that, that one

imb·er –ris m rain

imperāt·or –ōris m commander, emperor

imper·ō 1 w dat to command; imperārem I might command

improb·ō 1 to disapprove of, to condemn

imput·ō 1 to charge

in prep w abl in, on; w acc into

in mātrimōnium dūcere to lead (a woman) into marriage, to marry

in memoriā tenēre to remember

incrēsc·ō –ere incrēvī –– to grow, to increase

Īnfern·a –ōrum n pl the Underworld

inimīc·us –ī m enemy

inop·s –is wanting, lacking

īnsequ·ēns –entis next, following

īnsul·a –ae f island

intellegēns gen intellegentis intelligent, understanding

intellegenti·a –ae f understanding

intentē adv earnestly

intr·ō 1 to enter

inūtil·is –e useless

inveni·ō –īre invēnī inventum to find; inveniet he will find

Iōn·as –ae m Jonah

Iōsēph·us –ī m Joseph

Ioshu·a –ae m Joshua

ipsum pron yourself

īrācund·us –a –um angry

Isrāēl indecl Israel

iterum adv again

iubērem I might command

iūni·or –us younger

iūst·us –a –um just; n pl iūsta just things

iuven·is –e young; m young man

iuvent·a –ae f youth

iūxtā adv near, beside

labōr·ō 1 to work

lac lactis n milk

laet·us –a –um happy

latibul·um –ī n den

latr·ō –ōnis m robbers

laud·ō 1 to praise

lau·s –dis f praise

legūm·en –inis n vegetable

le·ō –ōnis m lion

Lēvīt·a –ae *m* Levite

lex lēgis *f* law

li·ber –brī *m* book

līber·ī –ōrum *m pl* children

līber·ō 1 to set free

line·us –a –um of linen

lingu·a –ae *f* language, tongue

litter·a –ae *f* letter of the alphabet; *pl* letters, literature

loc·us –ī *m* place

longinqu·us –a –um far off, distant

lūd·us –ī *m* play, game

lup·us –ī *m* wolf

luxuri·a –ae *f* luxury

magis *adv* more

magn·us –a –um large, great

malign·us –a –um stingy, malicious

mal·us –a –um bad, evil

mandāt·um –ī *n* command, commandment

man·us –ūs *f* hand

mar·e –is *n* sea

marīt·us –ī *m* husband

mē *pron* me; **mēcum** with me

me·us –a –um my; *voc* **mī**

Mēd·ī –ōrum *m pl* Medes, ancient people of the Middle East

medi·us –a –um middle of

medicīn·a –ae *f* medicine

mel mellis *n* honey

melior melius better

Melit·a –ae *f* island of Malta

mēns·a –ae *f* table

mēnsis mēnsis *m* month

Methodi·us –ī *m* Methodius, brother of Cyril and Apostle to the Slavs

mīl·es –itis *m* soldier

minis·ter –trī *m* attendant, helper

ministr·ō 1 to serve, to minister to, to execute, to carry out

misericordi·a –ae *f* kindness, mercy, pity

mitt·ō –ere mīsī missum to send

modesti·a –ae *f* restraint, discretion

moll·is –e gentle

molliter *adv* gently

mōn·eō –ēre –uī –itum to advise, to warn

mōn·s –tis *m* mountain

mōnstr·ō 1 to show; **mōnstrem** I may show

Moravi·a –ae *f* Moravia, region in Central Europe, part of the present day Czech Republic

mor·s –tis *f* death

mortuus est he died; **mortuus** dead

mōs moris *m* custom, habit, usual standard of behavior

mox *adv* soon

Moyses *indecl* Moses

mult·us –a –um much *pl* many; **multō** by much

mūr·us –ī *m* wall

Nabūchodonos·or –oris *m* Nebuchadnezzar, King of Babylon

namque *conj* for

nārr·ō 1 to tell, to tell about

nātālis nātālis *m* birthday

nat·ō 1 to swim

nāt·us –a –um born

naufrag·ium –ī *n* shipwreck

nāvigāti·ō –nis *f* sea-voyage

nāvig·ō 1 to sail

nāvis nāvis *f* ship

nec *adv* not; **nec . . . nec** neither . . . nor

necessit·ās –ātis *f* necessity

negle·gō –gere –xī –ctum to neglect

negōt·ium –ī *n* business

nēm·ō –inis *m* no one, nobody

Nīcolā·us –ī *m* Nicholas

nīd·us –ī *m* nest

nihil *indecl* nothing

Ninev·ē –ēs *f* Nineveh, the ancient capital of Assyria; *acc* **Ninevēn**

nōbīscum with us

noc·eō –ēre –uī –itum *w dat* to injure, to harm

nōlō nōlle nōluī to be unwilling, to not want; **nōlī** *w infin* don't

nōm·en –inis *n* name

nōn *adv* no, not

nōn numquam *adv* sometimes

nōn sōlum . . . sed etiam *conj* not only . . . but also

nōs *pro* we, us

nost·er –ra –rum our

nov·us –a –um new

nox noctis *f* night

nūb·ēs –is *f* cloud

num *conj* whether

numm·us –ī *m* coin (in this case, the sesterce)

numquam *adv* never

Nun *indecl* Nun

nunc *adv* now

nūnti·us –ī *m* messenger, message

nūper *adv* recently

nūtrīx nūtrīcis *f* nurse

occid·ēns –entis *m* the west

occīd·ō –ere –ī occīsum to kill

offic·ium –ī *n* duty, function, service

ōlim *adv* once

omn·is –e everyone; *pl* everything, all

oper·a –ae *f* work

oppugn·ō 1 to attack

Optimātēs political party of the Roman aristocrats

optim·us –a –um best

ōrāti·ō –ōnis *f* speech, manner of speaking, eloquence

ori·ēns –entis *m* the East

ōr·ō 1 to entreat

ostend·ō –ere –ī ostentum to show; **ostendentī** showing

ov·is –is *f* sheep

paenitenti·a –ae *f* repentance

pānis pānis *m* bread

Pannoni·a –ae *f* Pannonia, Roman province, an area roughly corresponding to Hungary

paralytic·us –a –um paralyzed

parēns parentis *m* parent

par·ō 1 to prepare

part·iō –īre –īvī –ītum to share

parv·us –a –um small, young; **parvulus** youngest

passer passeris *m* sparrow

pater patris *m* father

paterfamiliās patrisfamiliās *m* head of the household; *lit* father of the family

patiēns *gen* patientis patient, tolerant

patri·a –ae *f* fatherland, country

paup·er –era –erum poor

pāx pācis *f* peace

pecc·ō 1 to sin

pecūni·a –ae *f* money

perīcul·um –ī *n* danger

perrārō *adv* very rarely

Pers·ae –ārum *m pl* Persians

persecūti·ō –ōnis *f* persecution

perst·ō –āre –– to stand firm, to persist

pet·ō –ere petīvī petītum to seek, to ask, to request

Pet·rus –rī *m* Peter

Philisthīn·us –ī *m* Philistine

piet·ās –ātis *f* virtue, godliness

Pīlāt·us –i *m* Roman governor of Judea

pisc·is –is *m* fish

plac·eō –ēre –uī –itum *w dat* to please, to be pleasing to

plēn·us –a –um full, filled with

pōn·ō –ere posuī positum to put, place

Populārēs political party of the Roman common people

popul·us –ī *m* tribe or people

porc·us –ī *m* hog, pig

porti·ō –ōnis *f* share

port·ō 1 to carry, to bring; **portāns** carrying

possibil·is –e possible

post *prep w acc* after

postquam *conj* after, when

potest mūtārī is able to be changed

potest·ās –ātis *f* power

praecipu·us –a –um special, particular; **praecipuē** especially

praedīc·ō –ere praedīxī praedictum to predict, to command beforehand

praefic·iō –ere –fēcī –fectum *w dat* to put (someone *acc*) in charge of

praeter·eō –īre –īvī –itum to pass by

prex precis *f* prayer

preti·um –ī *n* value, price

prīmum *adv* first, in the beginning, at first

prīm·us –a –um first

prīn·ceps –cipis *m* chief, leader

prō *prep w abl* for, on behalf of, before, for

procul *adv* far off, at a distance

prō·iciō –icere –iēcī –iectum to cast away, to throw forth

prōnūnti·ō 1 to proclaim

prophēt·a –ae *m* prophet

propter *prep w acc* on account of, because of

prō·sum –desse –fuī –– *w dat* to be good for

prūdēns *gen* prūdentis careful, discreet

psall·ō –ere –ī to play the harp

puell·a –ae *f* girl

puer puerī *m* boy

pugn·ō 1 to fight

pul·cher –chra –chrum handsome, beautiful, good-looking

pulv·is –eris *m* dust

pūni·ō –īre –īvī –itum to punish

pūr·us –a –um pure; **pūra** pure things

quadrāgintā *indecl* forty

quaer·ō –ere quaesīvī quaesītum to seek, to ask; **quārēns** seeking

quam *in comparisons* than

quam frūctuōsissimum as fruitful as possible

quamquam *conj* although

quandō *conj* when

quasi *adv & conj* just as, just like, as if

–que (*syllable added at the end of a word to link it with the previous word*) and

quī quae quod *pron* who, which; he (she) who; **quae** (things) which

quia *conj* because

quīdam quaedam quiddam a certain person, a certain thing

quiēt·us –a –um quiet, tranquil

quīnque *indecl* five

quisquis quidquid whoever, whatever

quod *conj* because

rārō *adv* rarely

recip·iō –ere recēpi receptum to receive

recumb·ō –ere recubuī –– to recline at table with

refug·ium –ī *n* refuge

reg·ō –ere rēxī rēctum to rule

rēgīn·a –ae *f* queen

regn·um –ī *n* kingdom, royal power, rulership

relinqu·ō –ere **relīquī relictum** to leave, to leave behind, to abandon

remane·ō – ēre **remānsī** –sum to stay, to remain

rēs reī *f* thing, matter, event

respond·eō –ēre **respondī respōnsum** to respond

reven·iō ere revēnī reventum to return; **reveniam** I shall come

rēx rēgis *m* king

rīp·a –ae *f* riverbank

rog·ō 1 to ask

Rōm·a –ae *f* Rome

Rōmān·us –a –um Roman

rūf·us –a –um red, ruddy, having a healthy complexion

sac·er –ra –rum sacred, holy; **sacerrimus** most sacred

sacerd·ōs –ōtis *m* priest

saepe *adv* often

sānct·us –a –um holy; *n pl* **sancta** holy things

Sānctus Nīcolāus Sānctī Nīcolāī *m* Saint Nicholas

sangui·s –nis *m* blood, race

sapiēns *gen* **sapientis** wise

sapienti·a –ae *f* wisdom

satis *adv* enough

satrap·a –ae *m* governor, viceroy

Sa·ūl –ūlis *m* Saul

sc·iō –īre –īvī –ītum to know, to understand

schol·a –ae *f* school

scrīb·ō –ere **scrīpsī scriptum** to write

scienti·a –ae *f* knowledge

scrīpt·or –ōris *m* writer

Scrīptūr·a –ae *f* a writing, holy writing

secund·us –a –um second, following, next

sed *conj* but

sed·eō –ēre –ī **sessum** to sit; **sedēns** sitting

semper *adv* always

senect·ūs –ūtis *f* old age

senex senis *m* old man

sepulchr·um –ī *n* grave, tomb

serv·iō –īre **servīvī servītum** *dat obj* to serve; **servīte** *imp* serve

serv·ō 1 to save, to preserve

serv·us –ī *m* servant, slave

sevēr·us –a –um strict, severe

sext·us –a –um sixth

sī *conj* if

sibi *pron* for oneself

sīcut *conj* just like

siliqu·a –ae *f* husk

silv·a –ae *f* forest

Sim·ōn –ōnis *m* Simon

simil·is –e similar, like

similiter *adv* likewise, similarly

simplex *gen* **simplicis** simple, plain

sīmus we may be

sine *prep w abl* without

Sion *indecl* City of Zion, Jerusalem

societ·ās –ātis *f* fellowship, alliance

soci·us –ī *m* partner, companion

sōl sōlis *m* sun

sol·ium –ī *n* throne, chair

sōl·us –a –um alone, only

somn·ium –ī *n* dream

sor·or –ōris *f* sister

sors sortis *f* lot, decision by lots; **sortīre** to cast lots

spect·ō 1 to observe, to watch, to look at

speculāt·or –ōris *m* spy

spīrit·us –ūs *m* spirit

spoli·ō 1 to rob

stabulāri·us –ī *m* manager of a stable or lodging

stabul·um –ī *n* stable, simple lodging

statim *adv* at once, immediately

st·ō –āre stetī statum to stand

studiōs·us –a –um enthusiastic, interested; **studiōsus discendī** interested in learning

substanti·a –ae *f* wealth, property

sum esse fuī futūrum I am, to be

super *prep w acc* above, upon

super·sum –esse –fuī –futūrus to be left over, to survive

suprā *prep w acc* over, above

surg·ō –ere surrēxī surrēctum to rise

su·us –a –um his own, her own, its own

tam . . . quam as . . . as

tamen *adv* yet, nevertheless

tantum *adv* only, so great

taur·us –ī *m* bull

teg·ō –ere tēxī tēctum to cover; **tegentur** they will be covered

temp·us –oris *n* time

tempest·ās –ātis *f* storm

templ·um –ī *n* temple

tempt·ō 1 to try, to attempt

termin·ō 1 to mark the boundaries of

terr·a –ae *f* earth, ground, land

Tharsis *indecl* a city in Spain

Thessalonīc·a –ae *f* capital of Macedonia in northern Greece

tibi *pron* to you, for you

tim·eō –ēre –uī –– to fear, to be afraid; **timēte** *imp* fear

torquētur he is tortured

torr·eō –ēre –uī tōstum to scorch, to burn

tract·ō 1 to handle, to treat

trēs tria three

trīgintā *indecl* thirty

tū, tē *pron* you

tulit see **ferō**

tunic·a –ae *f* tunic, coat, garment

tu·us –a –um your

ubi *conj* when, where

umbrācul·um –ī *n* shade, shelter

ūn·us –a –um one

ung·ō –ere ūnxī ūnctum to anoint with oil

ūnivers·us –a –um all, whole, entire

urb·s –is *f* city

ūtil·is –e useful

ūtuntur *dep w abl* they use

uxo·r –ris *f* wife

vād·ō –ere vāsī –– to go

vās·um –ī *n* vessel, utensil

veni·ō –īre vēnī ventum to come; **venient** they will come

vent·er –ris *m* stomach, belly

vent·us –ī *m* wind

vēr·us –a –um true; *n pl* **vēra** things

verb·um –ī *n* word

vērit·ās –ātis *f* truth

verm·is –is *m* worm

vest·er –ra –rum your *pl*

ves·tis –tis *f* clothing, clothes

vet·ō –āre –uī –itum to forbid

vi·a –ae *f* road, path, way (method)

victōri·a –ae *f* victory

vide·ō –ēre vīdī vīsum to see

vinc·ō –ere vīcī victum to conquer

vincul·um –ī *n* chain, bond

vīne·a –ae *f* vine

vīn·um –ī *n* wine

vīper·a –ae *f* snake

vir virī *m* man

vīsi·ō –ōnis *f* apparition, vision

vīt·a –ae *f* life

vit·ium –ī *n* vice, bad habit, flaw, defect, fault

vīv·ō –ere vīxī vīctum to live, to be alive; **vīvendō** by living; **vīvēns** living

vōbīs *pron pl* to, for, by, with you

voc·ō 1 to call, to call upon; **vocārī** to be called

volō velle voluī to want, to wish; **vīs** you want, you wish

voluntāri·us –a –um voluntary

vor·ō 1 to swallow, to devour

vōs *pron pl* you

vuln·us –eris *n* wound, injury

vult·us –ūs *m* appearance, face

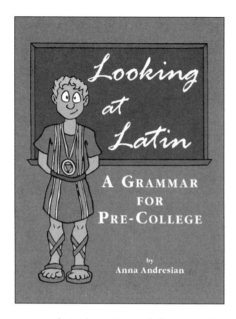

Looking at Latin
A Grammar for Pre-College
Anna Andresian

viii + 280 pp., 288 color illustrations (2006)
8½" x 11" Paperback, ISBN 978-0-86516-615-8

Looking at Latin is a complete illustrated grammar reference book for all levels of pre-college Latin.

Lessons cover single topics—which allows for flexibility in the order of presentation. Colorful visual elements bring clarity and energy to the presentation of grammatical material. Information delivered via text boxes allows students to use a step-by-step approach to learning, while comprehensive example sentences illustrate each topic in detail. Color illustrations add personality and humor, producing a visual appeal. Perfect review and reinforcement resource for Latin.

Looking at Latin
Online
Anna Andresian

Online subscription for *Looking At Latin*

The Most Comprehensive Latin Grammar Practice Site on the Internet

Anna Andresian's *Looking at Latin* visual grammar primer has been converted into review exercises for everything from first conjugation verbs to double datives and more. Some 10-to-50 self-correcting, illustrated questions accompany each topic.

Sign up today for a free, all-access, seven-day trial to review any point of grammar illustrated in *Looking at Latin*. Affordable annual subscriptions are priced per student or per school, for one year, or for several years.

No online resource has more ways to review the whole of Latin grammar, all in a contemporary, Flash-based interface, from the convenience of any computer in the world with an Internet connection.

WWW.BOLCHAZY.COM

The Original Dysfunctional Family

Basic Classical Mythology for the New Millennium

Rose Williams

x + 62 pp (2008)
6" x 9" Paperback, ISBN 978-0-86516-690-5

A very accessible introduction to classical mythology, *The Original Dysfunctional Family: Basic Classical Mythology for the New Millennium* presents the key stories of the twelve Olympians as well as those of the two gods associated with the fruits of the harvest, Demeter and Dionysus. The Greek version of each Olympian is presented first followed by the Roman adaptation. Chock-full of information, this book provides a sound foundation for the beginning student's further studies in culture, literature, and history. Students of all ages will find Williams' style engaging.

Features:

- Greek version of each Olympian followed by the Roman adaptation
- Genealogical charts of the Olympian family and their offspring
- Each set of stories presented in chronological order
- Notes section for Latin and other special terms employed in the text
- Illustrations drawn from the corpus of ancient sculpture

 WWW.BOLCHAZY.COM

The Clay-Footed SuperHeroes
Mythology Tales for the New Millennium
Rose Williams

(2009) 6" x 9"
Paperback, ISBN 978-0-86516-719-3

Designed for students unfamiliar with the classical world, *The Clay-footed Super-Heroes* provides a very accessible introduction to the SuperHeroes of classical mythology including such luminaries as Jason, Theseus, Heracles, Odysseus, and Aeneas. Student and general reader alike will enjoy Williams' wry sense of humor and her appreciation for the improbable. This book is an excellent text of manageable size and complexity for students beginning their study of literature, the humanities, or Latin and Greek.

Features:

- Narrative chronologically introduces the heroes, their families, and their adventures
- Special Note on the Roman counterparts to the Greek gods
- Glossary of Latin and special terms used in text
- Timeline of European history from the fifth century to the eighteenth
- 12 Black & White Illustrations
- Two Maps: Odysseus' Adventures & Aeneas' Journey to Rome

 WWW.BOLCHAZY.COM

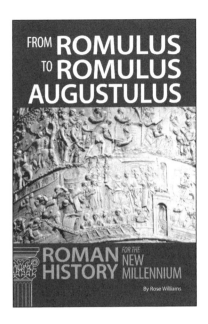

From Romulus to Romulus Augustulus

Roman History for the New Millennium

Rose Williams

(2009) 6" x 9"
Paperback, ISBN 978-0-86516-691-2

Readers will delight in the fascinating stories of Rome—the quirky, the gory, and the momentous. This book will serve as the perfect companion for the student beginning to study Latin or as an accessible introduction to Roman history for the general reader. Recognizing the symbiotic relationship between literature and the period in which it was produced, *From Romulus to Romulus Augustulus: Roman History for the New Millennium* provides a comprehensive overview of Roman history and Latin literature.

Features:

- Assessment of the critical events in Roman history
- Presentation of the key historical and literary figures of Rome
- Timeline of Roman history from its foundation to Theodoric
- Notes section for Latin and other special terms employed in the text
- Authentic illustrations from the Roman era

 WWW.BOLCHAZY.COM

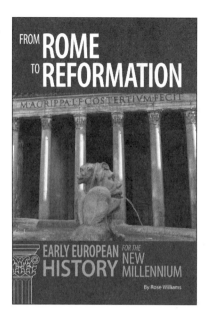

From Rome to Reformation

Early European History for the New Millennium

Rose Williams

(2009) 6" x 9"
Paperback, ISBN: 978-0-86516-718-6

Rose Williams skillfully leads the reader through the maze of power plays and the gradual rise of sovereign states that followed the collapse of the Roman Empire. Readers will appreciate Williams' engaging style and her ability to synthesize succinctly this busy period of history. Recognizing the symbiotic relationship between literature and the era in which it was produced, *From Rome to Reformation: Early European History for the New Millennium* provides a comprehensive overview of the interconnecting historical events, literary figures, and intellectual developments in European history and its Latin literature. This is a perfect companion text for courses in the humanities, western civilization, and Latin.

Features:

- Overview of the history of ideas developed in western civilization
- Assessment of the critical events in early European history
- Presentation of the key historical and literary figures of early Europe
- Timeline of European history from the fifth century to the eighteenth
- Notes section for Latin and other special terms employed in the text
- Illustrations enhance the text

WWW.BOLCHAZY.COM